Interactive
Non-Fiction and Media
11-14

Geoff Barton

www.heinemann.co.uk

✓ Free online support
✓ Useful weblinks
✓ 24 hour online ordering

01865 888080

Contents

Introduction

Welcome to *Interactive Non-Fiction and Media*. This course will help you explore the language, structure and style of a huge range of texts – from television commercials to autobiographies, from comedy scripts to websites.

The aim is to help you to develop your expertise in understanding the media. You live in a world which is very different from the one most of your teachers grew up in. Information is much more easily available. Communication is much faster. The power of the word has moved into unthought-of territories like blogs and podcasts.

The world can feel awash with information. The problem is knowing what's good and reliable, and what's untrue or inaccurate or downright dangerous.

That's why it is important to know as much as possible about how writers use language to communicate their message. Whether they are writing a speech or the home page of an internet site, we need to be as skilful as possible in looking at how their language works and what their meaning is.

Interactive Non-Fiction and Media is designed to do just that. It provides you with a range of different texts divided across six important genres or media areas:
- Newspapers
- Literary non-fiction (speeches, biography, diaries, etc.)
- Information and instructions
- Advertising
- TV and radio
- Film

In each section I have tried to choose texts that will interest you, sometimes amuse and entertain you and sometimes make you irritated or angry. Often there is a short text or activity to get you thinking about a particular media- or text-type. Then there is a longer text to explore in more detail.

The activities get you first to test your understanding – straightforward questions that let you check your knowledge. Then there are questions exploring the language and structure of texts, followed by activities that explore the wider issues.

The final activity gives you a chance to try creating part of a similar text for yourself – putting your knowledge into practical action.

There's also an introductory task – 'Getting started' – to lead you into each section, and an assessment task so you can show what you have learnt.

My hope is that you will enjoy the texts and activities, and through interacting with them become a more confident and more skilful reader and writer.

We live in an exciting and challenging knowledge-based world. Good luck in developing the skills you need to become a first-rate user of that knowledge.

Geoff Barton.

This unit explores how newspapers and magazines are written and published.

You will learn:

- how to write newspaper headlines
- how to write news and feature articles
- how to write for a specialist audience
- how to write a review
- how to write about sport.

1 Newspapers and magazines

Getting started

Make a list or spider diagram of key features of newspapers. Think about:

- how they are carried and stored
- how they use images
- how they give opinions
- what they contain apart from news.

1

Exploring newspaper headlines

You will learn:

- about the essential features of newspaper headlines
- how to write a good headline of your own.

The design of newspapers is important – it grabs the reader's attention. One essential ingredient is a good headline. This can be short and snappy, or may be quite long. But what it must do is quickly draw the reader in to the story.

Activity 1   Exploring newspaper headlines

It is usually the job of a newspaper or magazine sub-editor to read through a journalist's story and write a catchy headline.

1 What do you already know about newspaper headlines? Copy out the paragraph below, putting your own ideas in the gaps. In each gap you can write either just one word or a whole phrase.

Newspaper headlines are designed to _____ . A good newspaper headline is probably no more than _____ words long. It might be as short as _____ . Headlines are short and snappy because the sub-editors leave out words that are _____ .

2 Imagine there is a major fire at your school today. Tomorrow's newspapers will report the story. Look at the selection of headlines below. Choose the one that you think is (a) best and (b) worst. Then, for each one, explain what makes it a good or bad example of a headline. In your explanation, you might want to use words like:

- snappy
- pun
- dramatic
- exciting

- unexciting
- compressed
- present/past tense
- word-play

- brief
- long-winded
- jokey.

Set out your answer like this:

In my opinion the best headline is _____ because _____ .
I think the worst headline is _____ because _____ .

A — **Pupils flee burning school**

B — **School catches fire**

C — **Lots of staff and pupils run out of burning school**

D — **Classy fire**

E — **Lessons are abandoned as a fire grips a school**

F — **Major blaze grips school**

G — **School went up in flames**

H — **Lessons in firefighting**

I — **Really big blaze at local school**

J — **Fired up by learning**

Activity 2 Unpicking newspaper headlines

Think about any newspaper headlines you have seen recently. Did any grab your attention?

What are the ingredients of a good newspaper headline? Look at the list in the table below. For each one award a rating of 1–4:

1 = not important   3 = very important
2 = quite important   4 = essential

Find examples from the headlines below to illustrate these points.

Ingredients of a good newspaper headline	Rating 1–4	Example A–J
1 Written in the present tense.		
2 Refers to a person involved in the story (= human interest).		
3 Uses emotive words like 'crisis', 'victim', 'clash', 'fatal', 'fury'.		
4 Leaves out any unnecessary words like 'the' and 'a'.		
5 Aims to make the story sound dramatic.		
6 Uses alliteration (repeating letters at the start of words – e.g. 'football fury')		
7 Uses puns and word play (e.g. bad film review titled 'Star Bores')		

A Boy waits 29 hours for surgery
B Tributes to much-loved teacher
C Ready, steady, glow!
D Funding crisis hits charity project
E End of era for village garage
F Number of obese children is rising
G Woolworths sparks school uniform price war
H Two arrested over death of boy, 16
I Police hunt husband after stabbings
J 17m telly fans tune in to final

Activity 3 Writing headlines

Here is the opening of a newspaper story.

> After a barren 20 years, the patter of 10 pairs of little paws can be heard in the wolf enclosure at Colchester Zoo. Tallulah and Wilfy, a pair of timber wolves, are the proud parents of five cute little cubs, which are the first to be born for 20 years at Colchester Zoo.

1 Brainstorm three to five possible headlines for this story.

2 Choose the headline you like best. Then write a sentence explaining what you think makes it good.

Assess your progress

Look at the headlines you brainstormed for Activity 3 above. How many of the seven ingredients for good newspaper headlines have you included? (Remind yourself of these by re-reading the table in Activity 2.) Using labels and arrows or highlighting, show one example of each ingredient. If there are any ingredients you have not used, try to rewrite one of your headlines to include them.

2

Looking at news stories

You will learn:

- how to structure a news story
- more about the way journalists use language in news stories.

A good newspaper article starts by telling us the whole story. The first sentence is usually a topic sentence that tells us what happened, who was involved, where and when it occured. The rest of the story gives us more detail and eyewitness accounts.

Activity 1   Looking at a poorly written news story

Sometimes the best way to look at how something works is to analyse a bad model. Below is an example of how not to write a news story.

1 Read this newspaper article and list the things you think are wrong with it.

School meals are going to be shaken up a lot

By Mike Foley, Education reporter

There are new some new guidelines that were published yesterday and they are going to expect schools to change the kind of food and drink that they serve to pupils including banning certain types of food and drink such as sweet drinks and salty crisps.

'This is a good idea,' said Iain Veitch who is Headteacher at Wolverton Comprehensive School on the outskirts of Durham, just across the railway line.

Iain also said: 'I'm concerned at all the rubbish I see pupils eating and I think it's time we took a strong stand and gave a firm lead to pupils by banning food that will do them harm.'

The idea behind the guidelines is that there is a really big problem in Britain with children eating too much junk food and not doing enough exercise.

Meals that are high in salt and sugar won't be served any more. 'That's a good idea,' said pupil Sam Deeming who is in Year 9 and likes to eat crisps at break time.

The government announced its new proposals yesterday.

2 Imagine you are the editor of the newspaper. You have just received Mike Foley's article. How do you think he could improve it? What should he do about:

a) the headline

b) the overall structure of the article (i.e. the order of paragraphs)

c) the way he uses comments/quotations

d) the length of sentences – particularly in the first paragraph?

Activity 2 Advice for writing and improving articles

Sharpening up your style to write articles means understanding a few basic guidelines.

1 Read the advice given by journalist Julia Upton on how to write a good article.

- Make sure your first sentence tells the whole story – who, where, when. This is called a topic sentence.
- Keep paragraphs short – no longer than one or two sentences – so that they are easy to read in a hurry.
- Focus on the people in a story; this is what grabs a reader's interest.
- Use labels to give information about people (e.g. title, job, age).
- The early part of the article should tell the main story. The later parts add quotations and comments.

2 Take a look at how Julia re-writes the article from Activity 1. Look at the arrows pointing to key parts of the re-written story.

a) What is Julia doing that makes the story more interesting to read?

b) How could she improve the story further?

Chips face chop in school meal shake-up

Strict new government guidelines are about to change the nature of school dinners for ever.

Chips, pizza and stodgy puddings will become a thing of the past as strict new measures come into force.

The regulations aim to reverse the obesity trend of the past generation and educate pupils of all ages to think more carefully about what they eat. The ban covers vending machine sales of fizzy drinks, chips and confectionery.

Durham headteacher Iain Veitch, 44, commented: 'I'm concerned at all the rubbish I see pupils eating and I think it's time we took a strong stand by banning food that will do them harm.'

Assess your progress

Write two newspaper articles:

a) one completely ignoring Julia Upton's advice

b) the other following her advice as closely as possible.

Use arrows and labels around your articles to explain your decisions. You could write about:

- a new club that will soon be starting at your school
- a change in the rules or the uniform at your school.

3

Reading a newspaper article

You will learn:
- more about how a newspaper article is structured.

Whatever newspaper they are written for – national, local, serious, not-so serious – articles often follow a similar structure.

Activity 1 Understanding and interpreting an article

This *Daily Mail* article was written about unexpected summer weather conditions. Read it, then complete the activities.

1 Answer these questions to help you understand the text.

a) What is the name of the village that was first affected by the heavy rain?

b) How much later was the tornado spotted over Penzance?

c) Who took the photograph of the tornado?

d) How many firefighters cleared the mudslide?

And now today's weather: a mudslide and tornado

By Tom Kelly 18 August 2006

A county was struck by a mudslide and a tornado within the space of an hour as extreme storms ravaged Britain.

First a foot-deep deluge of soil and water swept through the village of Gulval, near Penzance in Cornwall during a torrential downpour.

Firefighters were called as the wall of mud surged down from a nearby field, blocking the main street and streaming into houses.

Forty minutes later, as the storm raged on, a tornado was spotted spinning over Penzance.

The whirlwind was captured on camera by property developer Adam Gibbard, as it made its way over buildings in the seaside town.

He said: 'It was all very quick. I was just shooting pictures of the cloud formations at the time, and when I saw it I just thought, "What's that?" It was like a tropical storm with lightning.'

Thankfully the tornado did not cause any damage, though the same could not be said of the mudslide, which took twelve firefighters several hours to clear up.

Eyewitness Rob Bowden said: 'There was a massive amount of mud. It washed down a field and flowed down the road.

'It went down towards people's houses and it was about a foot deep in the worst places.

'It ran down the sides of the houses and into back gardens.'

The Met Office reported other sightings of tornados in Lincolnshire and Warwickshire as storms lashed the country on Thursday afternoon.

The violent weather contrasted sharply with the baking heatwave most of Britain enjoyed last month. The south of England is currently enduring the worst drought for decades with millions of households suffering from hosepipe bans.

Yesterday *The Mail* told how a freak tornado in Baston, South Lincolnshire, hurled a steel cargo container into the air and dragged it along for 70 feet as five archaeologists sheltered inside.

Meanwhile a baby was thrown 10 feet across a bedroom after a bolt of lightning struck a home in Kidderminster, Worcestershire.

Kate Saunders, 26, and her one year-old son, Dylan, were sent flying when the thunderbolt struck the roof of their home, ripping every plug from its electric supply socket, and destroying the television, DVD player and video recorder.

Miss Saunders said: 'It was the most terrifying thing I had ever seen.

'One minute I was stripping the wallpaper, and the next myself and Dylan were blown across the room.

'It sounded like a bomb blast and there was a black mark left on my wall.'

The bad weather continued yesterday with heavy rain and thunderstorms across large swathes of the country.

Police in Doncaster said cars were left stranded in water on the main Bawtry Road route into the town centre and two houses in the nearby village of Finningley were damaged after being hit by lightning.

Paul Knightley, from PA WeatherCentre, predicted more thunderstorms across northern England and Scotland over the weekend. The south will see some sunshine, but this will also be interspersed with showers.

He said: 'It's going to be a mucky weekend, and there isn't likely to be an improvement in the weather until the middle of next week.'

Met Office meteorologist John Hammond said the combination of warm weather and short sharp showers had created ideal tornado conditions.

He said: 'Sunshine and showers, along with areas of low pressure nearby with warm ground that creates the rising air currents can lead to tornados.'

e) Where else were there reported sightings of tornadoes?

f) How else were people affected by the bad weather? Write down one example.

g) Who predicts that the weather will improve in the middle of next week?

2 Try these tasks, which will help you to interpret the text.

a) Look at the article headline.
   i) How is it different from many headlines in newspapers?
   ii) What do you think of it as a headline? (Write a sentence giving your response.)

b) Look at the opening topic sentence.
   i) Which of these 'W' questions does it answer? (Write down either the information or 'not applicable' if there is no information for the question.)
   - Where?   • When?   • What (happened)?   • Who?
   ii) Write a topic sentence for the story that gives some information for each question.

c) The article is written using very short paragraphs – many of them just one sentence long. How does this help readers to read the story?

d) The writer aims to make the story more dramatic with some of his choice of language. Look at the following examples and think of a less dramatic word he might have used than the one underlined.
   - 'storms <u>lashed</u> the country'
   - '<u>hurled</u> a steel cargo container into the air'
   - '<u>ripping</u> every plug from its electric supply socket
   - '<u>destroying</u> the television'

e) Study the comments of the two meteorologists. Which one uses more informal language? How can you tell?

Activity 2 Summarising the text

The news story in Activity 1 currently runs to about 580 words. Imagine the editor asks you to make it much shorter, because space is needed for another story. Re-write the article in 100 words. Use a combination of the original words and your own as you wish. Aim to keep the same structure, i.e.:
- topic sentence   • eyewitness/meteorologist comment.
- outline of main story and examples

Assess your progress

Which of these have you kept in your 100-word article?

A Headline
B Topic sentence
C Five examples of bad weather

D Comments, explanations and predictions from two experts
E Dramatic language

For each one, write one or two sentences explaining why you have kept it in or left it out of your article.

4

Comparing news articles

You will learn:
- how to compare the way two newspaper articles are written.

Different newspapers frequently contain the same news stories – except when they claim to have an 'exclusive' (a story that no other paper has). But the *way* the stories are written often varies.

In the past there were two types of newspaper: broadsheet (which had very large pages) and tabloid (which were much smaller in size).

Broadsheets, such as *The Times*, the *Telegraph* and the *Guardian*, were also known as the 'quality press'. Tabloids, such as the *Sun* and the *Mirror*, often 'sensationalised' the news through their use of language and photographs.

In recent years, some of the broadsheets have changed to a tabloid size, and many of today's papers carry similar stories about show business and celebrities.

On pages 13 and 14 you will find the same story (about British accents) from two newspapers: the *Mirror* and the *Guardian*. Use the tasks that follow these texts to compare the way they are written.

When it comes to comedy, accents are key

Sam Jones
Monday August 21, 2006

Like so many things in life, being funny would seem to be something of a postcode lottery. However, a team of boffins has trawled the country to discover how different accents influence how comical we find a person.

After asking 4,000 people to listen to the same joke in 11 different regional accents, researchers from the University of Aberdeen concluded that the Brummie accent, as typified by the likes of Frank Skinner, Jasper Carrott and Lenny Henry, is Britain's funniest, appealing to more than a fifth of those questioned.

The Scouse accent took second place, while the lilting tones of Geordies came third with 14.3% of the vote.

The Mancunian and Glaswegian accents fared less well, respectively tickling the funny bones of 2.1% and 3.4% of those polled.

Languishing at the bottom of the list was received pronunciation. The clear, rootless accent once favoured by BBC broadcasters, appealed to just 1.1% of participants.

The study also discovered that accents perceived as warm were deemed funnier than apparently cold ones, and that Cockney patter was particularly suited to risqué humour.

Dr Lesley Harbidge, the comedy expert who led the research, chose a test joke which reflected the traditions of British stand-up comedy and forced the listener to concentrate on the teller's pronunciation rather than their apparent cleverness. The researchers found that the three funniest accents – Brummie, Scouse and Geordie – were also deemed to be the least intelligent.

Text A: from the *Guardian*

Brummie twang is funniest

21 August 2006
By Graham Brough

Brummie is the funniest accent for joke telling - but also the most stupid sounding, a survey says.

The study revealed the twang associated with Birmingham comedians Jasper Carrott, Frank Skinner and Lenny Henry was the most comical.

Researchers told the same joke to 4,000 people in various accents, with Brummie chosen by 20 per cent as the funniest.

Liverpudlian, as spoken by comedians such as Ken Dodd and Paul O'Grady, came second with the Geordie accent of Ant and Dec third.

A posh accent was found to be the least humorous for joke-cracking by comedy expert Dr Lesley Harbidge for the paramount Comedy Channel survey.

And it was not all good news for those from Britain's second city as the Brummie twang was picked as sounding the least intelligent by 33 per cent of those questioned.

Yorkshire was voted the warmest accent by 25 per cent, followed by Welsh (15 per cent) and Geordie (13 per cent).

Text B: from the *Mirror*

Activity 1 Reading the same story in different newspapers

1   Answer these questions to help you understand the texts.

a) What is the name of the writer of each text?

b) How did researchers work out which accent was funniest?

c) What does Text A call the least funny accent?

d) According to Text B, which are the three funniest accents?

e) According to Text B, which accent is the least funny?

f) Which text tells you what comedy expert Lesley Harbidge's job is?

g) The reported survey looks at how funny we think different accents are. What else did it discover about our attitudes to different accents?

2 Interpret the texts using these tasks and questions.

a) Use the table to compare the complexity of each text.

	Text A: the *Guardian*	Text B: the *Mirror*
How many words are there in the headline?		
How many words are there in the first paragraph?		
How many words are there in the second paragraph?		
What words in the article do you *not* know or are *not* familiar with? List them.		
Which newspaper has more of these unfamiliar words?		

b) In general, the *Guardian* uses more complicated words and phrases than the *Mirror*. Think of some simpler words you could use instead of these:
- however
- reflected
- perceived
- deemed to be.

c) Does one of the articles tell you anything that the other doesn't? Use a table like the one below to help you list your findings.

Mirror	*Guardian*

d) Which headline do you prefer, and why?

e) Which version of the story do you prefer overall and why?

f) What could you say about the two different audiences which the writers are aiming at?

Assess your progress

Write down as many similarities and differences as you can between the articles in the *Mirror* and the *Guardian*. Think about:
- the news stories they choose
- the kind of information they include
- the language they use
- their headlines
- the audience they are writing for
- the intended purpose of their writing.

5

Looking at feature articles

You will learn:
• how to write feature articles.

People assume that newspapers are full of news stories. In fact, they contain many other types of articles too, including:

- interviews
- celebrity gossip
- opinion pieces in which a writer says what they think
- articles about gardening, entertainment, cookery
- advice
- in-depth articles that examine the background to the news.

Similarly, most magazines contain features articles about a range of subjects.

Activity 1 Exploring feature articles

1 Look at these newspaper cuttings, which contain opening sentences from different articles. For each one, decide whether it is a news or feature article.

A
You may be about to make a major purchase or investment.

B
Nearly 18,000 weapons were handed in during the first week of the national knives amnesty – including an anti-tank missile.

C
The new Porsche GT3 sports coupe will go on sale in Europe next month.

D
Government plans to build hundreds of thousands of new houses across Britain are a greater threat to the country's most at-risk species and habitats than climate change.

E
A few years ago I forced the chef John Torode to taste-test 80 supermarket-available organic products with me. I still wake sometimes in the middle of the night shaking in terror at the memory of that day, which has since infested my nightmares.

F

BRITNEY SPEARS has come out fighting and turned on her critics.

G

It was early Sunday morning when my family became yet another statistic as our house was broken into by thieves wielding an iron bar.

H

Whaling, by its very nature, is cruel. It also serves no useful purpose. So it should stop.

I

ENGLAND suffered another crushing defeat to Australia as the Wallabies ran up a 43–18 score to clinch the Cook Cup and the series 2–0 in Melbourne.

2 For each opening (A–I), decide whether you think it is written:

a) to entertain   b) to inform   c) to persuade.

3 Look at the list of text-types below.

a) For each opening, decide which text-type you think it might be.

b) Which type was easiest to decide on? Which type was hardest? Why do you think this was?

> **Text-types**
> - Opinion piece
> - Travel writing
> - Food writing
> - Sports report
> - News article
> - Review
> - Horoscope
> - Celebrity gossip
> - Interview
> - Leader article (in which the newspaper states the views of its editor)

Assess your progress

1 Swap your answers to Tasks 2 and 3a with a partner. Tick the answers you agree on and put a question mark by those you disagree on. Try to come to an agreement about all your answers – but remember, some text-types may have more than one purpose.

2 How good are you at identifying the purpose and text-type of a piece of writing?

☐ Expert   ☐ Not bad   ☐ Need more help

Activity 2   Getting started

The opening of a feature article is really important. It can hook readers into a subject they might not have thought they there were interested in. Journalists can sometimes be assigned stories they find boring, but they have to bring them to life.

1. Imagine being asked to write about one of these topics:
   - vending machines
   - public transport
   - Key Stage 2 tests.

How would you start your article? Often the best way is to try out lots of different openings to loosen up your brain. Write down three possible openings of one or two sentences in length.

Features writer Wynn Rees says ...

The key is to know your audience and to write directly to them. If you are writing an opinion piece on something they may not know about, use an attention-grabbing opening sentence, or tell a story that will catch their interest. Try to surprise your reader. Help your reader to visualise people and places – use description. Help them to hear the words a person says – use dialogue.

2 Read through these openings for an article on breakfast cereal packets. Which do you like best, and why?

A: Personal

I always like to have lots of cereal packets on the table. That way I can use them to block out the view of my family.

B: Dialogue

'You're late. You should be down here by now.' Breakfast time in our house always starts with an argument and a wildly over-designed breakfast cereal box.

C: Factual

Although our habits are changing, the British still love breakfast. After going 10-12 hours overnight without food energy, our reserves are low and our brains and bodies need fuel. Eating breakfast cereals apparently helps to keep our blood sugar levels stable throughout the morning and helps us to function more effectively. But just how are cereals produced, and why do we seem much keener to eat them than, say, the French or the Italians?

D: Descriptive

A plain white bowl, a neatly piled stack of wheaty square things, like bales of hay, and milk splashing wildly – then they have the cheek to write 'serving suggestion' at the side. How else do they think we'd serve our cereal – on the table? In the dog's dish? Smothered in salt?

Activity 3 Writing a feature article

You are about to write the opening paragraph of an article. You can choose your own topic – e.g. something you already know about such as a hobby or interest, a style of music or band you like, or a sport you play or watch. Try to write in a style you haven't tried before.

Here are some tips to help.
- Write various drafts first. Experiment with using description, facts, dialogue, a personal tone.
- Decide whether you want the purpose of your article to inform, to entertain, or something else.
- Based on that decision, choose the opening you think is most effective. Remember: think about how you hook the interest of your reader.

Assess your progress

Either by writing four or five sentences, or by using arrows and labels, explain how the opening paragraph of your article:
- achieves the purpose you intended
- grabs your reader's interest.

6

Reading a feature article

You will learn:
- to read a feature article in more detail.

Feature articles come in all shapes and styles, covering any subject you can think of. Sometimes they fill in the background to the news, as this article on bird flu shows.

Activity 1   Studying information in feature articles

Read this feature article from *The Newspaper*, which is published six times a year especially for school students.

---

*Health*News

Flu and you

We humans love to scare ourselves. Newspapers and TV news are full of shock-horror stories about the killer flu virus but are there things we can do to cut our risk of catching it?

Every year, people in Britain catch the flu virus and some of those who are already ill, or are very young or very old, may die.

It is very sad, but modern treatment means that many deaths can be avoided.

Global diseases, or epidemics like flu that spread around the world, are called pandemics.

The worst of these was the Black Death of 1349, also known as the bubonic plague, that killed 75 million people worldwide.

Bird flu on the way

Experts tell us that the world is due another flu epidemic and that the latest bird-flu virus would be the most likely cause.

However, the chances of most of us catching bird flu and dying are very small indeed.

Humans can catch the disease only after close contact with a sick bird. However, if someone who had normal flu were to come into contact with bird flu, this could be very dangerous.

The bird flu virus could attach itself to the human flu virus, mutate and then start to spread from person to person.

How to protect yourself

Coughs and sneezes always have spread diseases, especially colds and flu, and they still do.

If bird flu does begin to infect humans, it will spread through coughs and sneezes.

The spray from a sneeze can travel at 80mph and droplets can land 10 metres away. Just one sneeze can project 100,000 flu germs into the air.

Use your hankie

If you want to stay free of flu and someone coughs or sneezes at you, what should you do?

First, keep your hands away from your face and wash them and your face as soon as you can.

Flu germs enter through the nose, mouth and eyes.

If a cough or sneeze spray misses your face and you accidentally touch a droplet with your hands and then touch your face, the flu or cold bug could creep into your system.

Always cough and sneeze into a handkerchief. Don't go out without one or if you do – leave your nose at home!

1 Answer these questions to help you understand the article.
   a) What facts are given in this article? Write down three.
   b) How can humans catch bird flu?
   c) What could happen to the bird flu virus that would make it much more dangerous?
   d) What does the article suggest if someone coughs or sneezes at you?
   e) What does the article suggest if you are coughing and sneezing?

2 Use these questions to help you interpret the text.
   a) The article aims to give us information plus advice.
      ● Write down an example of a sentence that informs.
      ● Write down an example of a sentence that persuades or advises.
   b) Look at the headline. If this had been a news article reporting an outbreak of bird flu it would probably be more urgent and dramatic. Think of a headline that might accompany a news report.
   c) Look at the opening three sentences of the article. What is surprising about the way the writer says 'It is very sad'?
   d) How do the three subheadings (e.g. 'Bird flu on the way') help the reader to read the article?
   e) Who is the writer of this text aiming it at?

3 The article is written in quite an informal way, but it also uses technical language. Find some examples of:
   ● an informal everyday word or phrase
   ● a technical or scientific word
   ● a statement
   ● an instruction.

   For each of these, write a sentence that explains:
   a) why you think the writer chose to use them
   b) how they suit the writer's intended audience.

4 Write two or three sentences giving your response to this article. Include what you like about it and what you dislike about it.

Assess your progress

What are the most important things that writers of feature articles need to remember? Look back at your work on Sections 5 and 6, then write down all the things to remember. Finally, choose five things you feel are essential for success.

7

Writing for a specialist magazine

You will learn:

• how to write for a specialist audience.

Mainly, newspapers are aimed at a general audience. This means that anyone might read them, whatever their age or gender. Magazines often have more specialist audiences. Some might aim themselves at people of a certain age (e.g. women aged 16–24). Others might aim at people with a particular interest (e.g. BMX, computer games, fishing).

Writing for a specialist audience means your readers already know about the subject. Therefore, they will probably expect your writing to be more technical and advanced than in a general publication.

Activity 1 Exploring specialist writing

Read paragraphs A–F, which are all about keeping fish. Some are written for a general audience; others are taken from specialist magazines. Try to work out which is which. In particular look for:

• technical terms, statistics, factual style (specialist)
• familiar words, storytelling, informal style (general).

A

It's a fish!' we chorused. Yes, there's no faulting our powers of observation. In fact, it's a goldfish with a few black splodges to add character to its otherwise golden appearance. 'I think it's time you lot learnt a bit about responsibility,' said the boss.

B

Two species of wobbegong shark have been redescribed, with one species previously believed to be a synonym, raised to species level once again. Charlie Huveneers from Macquarie University in Australia redescribed *Orectolobus ornatus* and *O. halei* based on new specimens caught from temperate waters off eastern Australia and has just published his findings in the journal *Zootaxa*.

C

Goldfish are set to be banned as fairground prizes under new animal welfare laws. Stall owners who give away fish, rabbits and other animals would face up to a year in jail. Leaked notes on the Government's draft animal welfare bill stress that people thinking about owning a pet should consider the animal's welfare. The notes add: 'It would be inconsistent with this aim for an animal ever to be a prize.' The legal shake-up would also ban kids under 16 from buying some types of pets including cats, dogs and goldfish.

D

In terms of size, all things are relative, and although reef hobbyists do have success with micro reef systems down to as small as $45\,^1/_{10}$ gal, these are usually refugiums attached to much larger reef tanks or tiny specialist systems for keeping limited types of subjects such as seahorses or mini invertebrates. A fully fledged mixed reef community system needs to be much larger, and I would recommend, as a minimum, no smaller than $230\,^1/_{50}$ gal.

E

Fishkeeping experts say tap water isn't good for pond fish, but rain water is. The problem is often how to get it into the pond, as even a good shower doesn't fill it up. My mate Mike, a landscape gardener, got me thinking when I was mulling over the problem with him the other day.

F

A large marine fish in an exhibit in a Chinese public aquarium has died after becoming grossly overweight from eating kilos of fish every day. A diet of 10 kg/22 lbs of fresh fish every day saw the grouper at Beihai Sea World in south China's Guangxi Zhuang Autonomous Region grow from a size of just 30 cm/12 in to a massive 150 kg/330 lbs and around 1.6 m/5 ft 4 in just five years.

Write your response like this:

Text _____ is from a general/specialist publication. The two main clues in the text are _____ and _____

Activity 2 Reading a specialist article

This article comes from *Mountain Biking UK*. Read the first part and explore the clues that tell you it is a specialist magazine.

FROM PARK TO TRAIL

Chris Smith loves riding skateparks, but park is a BMX thing. Britain's most versatile rider shows you how to take those skills and make them work in the great outdoors...

Chris Smith goes into a trance when he rides skateparks – sprint, blunt, hop, pump, barspin, tap, hip, repeat. He can't help it. Once he's in the zone the riding becomes a seamless progression of moves. See ramp, ride it – a dozen different ways. It's a pleasure to watch.

But just lately, if you'd been a fly on the wall – or ramp – you might have heard some muttering. Chris isn't the kind of rider who normally complains about riding, but he's got something that he needs to get off his chest.

The gist of his complaint? It's the kind of viewpoint that's sure to set off heated forum debates, but Chris has a point. Skateparks, after all, are about BMXs and skateboards, natch. Mountain bikers have just nicked the venue and most of the moves. Park riding is great to watch and fun to do, but it ain't mountain biking. Which got Chris thinking: why not take some of the skills and moves from riding park and transfer them to somewhere more suitable for mountain bikes?

1 Answer these questions to help you understand the text.
   a) Re-read the opening paragraph. What will this article explain to the reader?
   b) Why does Chris Smith not cycle at skate parks?
   c) What does the writer mean by 'natch' (final paragraph)?
   d) What does the writer think are the positive things about park riding?

2 Use these tasks and questions to help you interpret the text.
   a) How can you tell that the text is aimed at mountain bike enthusiasts rather than general readers?
   b) What do you learn about Chris Smith's skills as a cyclist?
   c) What do you learn about his attitude to skate-parks?
   d) What can you tell about the writer's attitude to Chris Smith's riding skills? Write down three words or phrases that show this.
   e) Write down one sentence from the article in which the writer informs the reader.
   f) Write down one sentence in which the writer describes something for the reader.
   g) For each of the four paragraphs in the opening to this article, write a short sentence that sums up what it is about.
   h) Would this article make you want to read on? In a sentence explain why or why not.

Activity 3 Writing for a specialist audience

Choose a hobby or interest (music, sport or cinema perhaps) and think about a star or expert in that area. It could be a singer, athlete or actor. Write an article for a specialist magazine that profiles this person and describes their work.

Remember …
- The purpose of your article is to inform and describe. What information will you include? What will you describe?
- Plan what you will put in each paragraph before you start writing.
- Make your opinion of your subject clear to the reader. What words or phrases will you use to show this?
- Your readers are fellow fans – so you can use some technical language and don't need to explain basic information to them.

Assess your progress

Look again at the article you have written. Use labels and arrows to show where you have included:
- information
- description
- a clear idea of your opinion of the subject of your article
- some technical or specialist language.

Looking at reviews

You will learn:
- about the language of reviewing.

A regular feature of most newspapers is reviewing films, CDs, plays and concerts. This isn't as easy as it sounds. Often you will be writing for readers who haven't heard or seen the performance, so you need to be able to entertain them.

Activity 1 Examining a bad review

A good way of learning how to write good reviews is by exploring bad ones. Look at this review of Robbie Williams' *Greatest Hits* album. Why is this such a bad review?

1 What advice would you give to this reviewer about the following?
- The choice of words – e.g. 'good' and 'great'.
- The use of the personal pronoun 'I'.
- The structure of the article.

2 Write a better opening sentence for the review. Think about how this sentence could give:
- background information on the subject
- details about the album being reviewed
- an opinion on the artist (before actually reviewing the album).

Is there anything else you could include?

> I listened all the way through to Robbie Williams' *Greatest Hits* album and to be absolutely honest with you I didn't like it as much as I had expected to. There are lots of songs on there that I've heard my mum and dad singing along to, but I didn't think they sounded that great when I listened to them on my own. Robbie is meant to be a really good performer when he performs live, but I wasn't so impressed when I just listened to the songs on this album. Mind you, 'Angels' is a classic and I liked that.

Activity 2 Examining a review

Here is a review of Robbie Williams' *Greatest Hits* written for BBC online by Talia Kraines.

REVIEW

From the tender beginnings of Take That – complete with lycra shorts and 'interesting' dance routines – Robbie Williams has worked his way into the hearts and onto the bedroom walls of the nation. After thirteen years we now have this, his greatest hits album, cataloguing his journey from the teenage heartbreak of leaving Take That through to the Robbie we know so well.

After five studio albums, this compilation isn't going to hold any surprises. It's worth noting that Robbie isn't one of those artists whose singles are great but the rest of the album isn't much cop.

While *Sing When You're Winning* probably clocks in as the weakest of the albums, each one is a great listen in itself, and this compilation is perhaps somewhat weaker for containing singles only, missing strong album tracks like *I've Been Expecting You*'s fiery 'Karma Killer' and *Life Through A Lens*' romping 'Ego A Go Go'.

We kick off with the first single from *LTAL*, the laddish 'Old Before I Die'. The now classic (and somewhat overrated) 'Angels' is promoted out of chronological order to track 2 and will undoubtedly be a highlight of the album for many. For me, however, it's the other ballads that are the stand-out tracks.

1. What is the writer's aim in the first paragraph of this review?

2. What does she mean when she writes that 'Robbie Williams has worked his way into the hearts and onto the bedroom walls of the nation'?

3. What phrases does the writer use that are factual, rather than expressing an opinion?

4. Which words and phrases tell us her opinion? Pick out some examples.

5. In the last paragraph, the writer gives her opinion on specific tracks from the album. Why is it important that she does this?

6. What does she think overall of the album? Does she like it? How can you tell?

Activity 3 Writing a review

A good review of a film, play, CD or restaurant will:
- entertain the reader, perhaps with a quirky and memorable use of language
- give background facts or information
- describe the subject, so even if the reader hasn't seen, heard or tasted it, the reviewer helps them to imagine it
- pick out specific details – particular actors, songs or ingredients – and give an opinion on them
- give the reviewer's overall opinion towards the end of the review, not usually in the first sentence
- use a range of words instead of just 'good' or 'bad'.

Choose one of these topics and write the opening paragraph of a review.
- a meal you have recently had (including a school lunch)
- an album you like or dislike
- a film you have recently seen
- a concert or performance you attended.

hints

The first sentence or paragraph of anything can often seem the hardest to write. A good starting point for your review might be to:

- use a quotation, fact or statistic (e.g. 'Three million people in America saw this movie in one weekend alone. I'm glad I wasn't one of them …')
- use description ('The crowd was getting impatient after a 35-minute delay caused by a sound fault …').

Assess your progress

Look again at your review. Then look at the six bullet points at the start of Activity 3, which list the ingredients of a good review. Have you achieved all of these in your own review? Use arrows and labels to show where you have, and to show the changes you can make to include all of them.

9

Comparing reviews

You will learn:
- to compare the way reviewers make their judgements.

Like all of us, different reviewers have their own tastes and opinions. One reviewer might really like a certain film, book or restaurant, while another may dislike them all. Reviewers also tend to write in their own individual style.

Activity 1 Exploring opinions and style

Here's a collection of newspaper reviews gathered together from *The Week* magazine. Explore the differences in the reviewers' opinions and style using the activities that follow.

New cars: what the critics say

BMW 3-Series Coupé 335i
Price: £33,420

Autocar
The new 3-Series is a "very polished product" with attractive lines, six gears and a 0-60mph time of 5.5 seconds. It also has a boot large enough to fit two golf-bags and several suitcases. Drivers and passengers both get plenty of leg- and head-room and the "bucket-like" seats are pleasingly comfortable. But although it performs well at most speeds – and it is "extremely fast" – it feels rather "harsh" to drive.

The Times
BMW has tried to be "conservative" with the styling of the new 3-Series, but has ended up just being "bland". There is some purpose to the front, but the side is "oddly proportioned and the back verging on the insipid". On the road, however, it's a different story. The engine is turbocharged, and offers a fast (top speed: 155mph), "thrilling" and "exceedingly firm" ride.

Auto Express
This slick, "head-turning" machine is the "most civilised two-door money can buy". True enthusiasts will love its "blistering performance and pin-sharp handling", while drivers with more aesthetic requirements will revel in its "rakish looks". Clever design flourishes include sleek wing mirrors, bespoke headlamps and LED tail lights. Inside, the cockpit is "snug" with plenty of useful gadgets.

The best... running shoes

Adidas 1.1 This new, super-high-tech trainer from Adidas has a mini-computer hidden in the sole, which apparently makes 1,000 calculations per impact to determine the precise degree and distribution of cushioning you need. It's a comfortable shoe, but not much more comfortable than other, less expensive models. Price: £175 (0870-240 4204; www.adidas.co.uk).

Asics Gel Kinsei The Gel Kinsei is Asics's "most technologically advanced shoe", and a very good buy. Packed with innovative features, including a special gel-filled heel to minimise jarring, it is designed to suit most running styles. It is also "extremely comfortable" from the first time of wearing. Price: £130 (01925-243360; www.asics.co.uk).

Nike Air Max 360 The classic Nike Air Max may look "more street than track", but don't underestimate it. The shock-dampening unit ensures that you run on a "cushion of air", but its main benefits are "stability" and "durability". On the downside, it feels rather "plasticky" on the street and has an "irritatingly short" tongue. Price: £120 (0800-056 1640; www.nike running.com).

Mizuno Wave Creation 7 The USP of this shoe is the "wave plate technology" in the sole, which disperses the impact when the foot hits the ground. Primarily designed for runners with high arches, who require extra protection on hard surfaces, the shoe feels "flat and stiff", which takes some getting used to. Price: £90 (www.mizunoeurope.com).

Asics Gel Noosa Tri This purpose-built triathlon running shoe is very light (300g), with a "supersoft" lining and a breathable open-mesh upper. A great 10km shoe for fast-tempo training or races. The fluorescent colours may not be to every-one's taste, but they will make you stand out on dark evenings. Price: £85 (as before).

SOURCE: THE SUNDAY TELEGRAPH

1 Answer these questions about the car reviews.

   a) Write down a positive comment about the BMW from the *Times*.

   b) Write down a negative comment from *Autocar*.

   c) Count how many positive comments each of these three reviews makes.

   d) Count how many negative comments each of them makes.

2 Answer these questions to help you interpret the car reviews.

   a) Which review do you think is the most positive?

   b) Which do you think is the most negative?

   c) Which review do you think is the most balanced?

   d) Which review do you think is the most interesting?

   e) Which do you think is the most difficult to understand?

3 Read all five shoe reviews.

   a) Write down three things the writer thinks are important when choosing a pair of running shoes. For each of these three things, write down an example from any one of the reviews.

   b) Note down the review that you think is the most negative and the review you feel is most positive. For each of these, write a sentence or two explaining your decision.

   c) If someone said: 'If I want to buy something, I just buy it – I don't need to read a review', how would you defend the need for reviews?

   d) As a buyer, which review do you find most useful? Explain why.

Activity 2   Write a review

Choose a product you know well (e.g. a games console or a mobile phone), then write a review of it. Think about the things that might be important to a reader when considering buying this product. Remember to refer to specific details or features of the product that you like or dislike.

You could structure your review as a sandwich. So, for example, if you are writing a mainly positive review:
- start with positive comments – what you like about the product
- explain one or two negatives – what you dislike about the product
- give your overall positive opinion.

Assess your progress

1 Ask a partner to read your review and answer these questions.

   a) Did the writer make it clear what they liked about the product?

   b) Did the writer make it clear what they disliked about the product?

   c) Did the review help you to decide whether to buy this product?

   d) What could the writer add to help you make up your mind?

2 Use your partner's answers to help you improve your review.

10

Looking at sports journalism

You will learn:
• how to write about sport.

Sports writing falls into two areas. First there is sports reporting, which describes a match or game, tells us how it was played and what the result was. Then there is sports writing, which takes a more general view – looking at a particular sport or game, telling us about a famous player, spotting trends and patterns in the game.

Activity 1 Exploring sports journalism

1 These days, we can watch live sport on the television and listen to commentaries on radio. So why do you think people still like to read sports reports in newspapers, even though they are published one or two days after the event? Which of these explanations do you *most* and *least* agree with?

A TV coverage is too fast. Newspapers allow you to take it at your own pace.

B Live coverage doesn't give the full analysis that writers can.

C Words can often paint a picture that is better than live footage.

D Newspaper reports are aimed at people who can't afford digital TV.

E Written reports give background and opinions as well as giving us scores.

F Sometimes it's good to read about an event as well as watching it live.

2 Here are three sports reports published in the *Daily Telegraph*. Look at the way each reports on an event.

WOODS GOES STRIDING ON

By Lewine Mair at Medinah

Tiger Woods ran away with his third PGA championship and the 12th major of his career here yesterday. Having made two killer putts of over 30 feet in his first eight holes, he had a closing 68 to finish at 18 under par and a yawning five shots clear of Shaun Micheel.

Text A

England's double triumph

By Richard Collins

England's women qualified for the Uber Cup world team finals for the first time in eight years by beating Denmark 3–0 in the European zone qualifying competition at Thessalonika.

Singles wins for Tracey Hallam and Elizabeth Cann, and doubles success for Gail Emms and Donna Kellogg, enabled England to beat Denmark on Saturday for the first time in fourteen years.

Text B

CAPIROSSI WIN HOTS UP TITLE RACE

By Dave Fern

Loris Capirossi powered relentlessly to victory in a Czech Republic round of the World MotoGP series that intensified the battle for the title as Valentino Rossi and Dani Pedrosa gained ground on the championship leader, Nicky Hayden.

Text C

Compare the reports using this bingo grid. For each comment the answer could be A / B / C / all / none.

Find a text that …

1 … uses dramatic language to grab our interest.	2 … makes the player sound like a hero.	3 …gives the writer's own opinion.
4 …uses some technical language.	5 … uses jokes or puns.	6 … tells us when the match or contest took place (e.g. 'yesterday').
7 …tells us what the sport was.	8 … gives us some history on how the team or player have done.	9 … tells us where the event took place.

3 Which of the features in the bingo grid could you identify? Use a copy of the table below to check which reading skills are a strength and which you need to develop. Which skill are you best at?

If you could find texts which showed:	… then you can …
6, 7, 8, 9	… find facts and information.
1, 2, 4, 5	… identify and comment on the language the writer uses.
3	… identify the writer's opinion.

Activity 2 Reading sports journalism

Sometimes sports journalists don't report on a particular match or game. Instead, they try to sum up a player or team style. This tells us more about what it is like to be, for example, a famous cricketer, footballer or tennis star.

Here's an example by Martin Amis, who writes a description of seven-times Wimbledon tennis champion, Steffi Graf.

Steffi Graf is something unbelievable on the tennis court, a miracle of speed, balance and intense athleticism. She looks like a skater but she moves like a puck. During changeovers she gets up early from her chair, and she is always exasperated (hands on hips, head bowed) by any delay, from her opponent or ball boy. After a great shot she doesn't wait for the applause to start, let alone stop, before she is striding back to the touchline, twiddling her racket like a six-gun. She never smiles. She wants to win every set to love and get on with the next one. You feel that the only player she would enjoy facing is herself.

Today she is facing Gabriela Sabatini, who has never beaten her in eleven meetings. And it looks like the same old story. Steffi's forehand is booming, and she is slicing her backhand under the breeze. Instead of retreating 20 feet for the high topspin (as Chris Evert had done in the semi-final), Steffi adopts the ploy of jumping waist-high to make her drives. Steffi is one set up and serving at 3–2 in the second. The crowd groans and sweats for the wilting, shamefaced Gaby. Then something happens.

And we'll never know what. Steffi collapses in a blizzard of errors, losing all but one of the next eleven games. An instant after the last point Gaby has the snout of a TV camera in her face. Then a microphone in her hand ('It's hard to talk right now'). Soon she is in the press tent, being asked what she feels ('It's hard to say'). And then she is packing her rackets and heading down to Key Biscayne for the Lipton, where she will lose to Mary Joe Fernandez in the quarters, and where Steffi, as tennis writers say, will return to her winning ways.

1 Read the text, then answer these questions.

a) What phrase or sentence shows Steffi Graf's determination to win? Choose one.

b) When the writer says that Graf looks like a skater but is more 'like a puck', what do you think he means?

c) The writer says that Steffi twiddles her racket 'like a six-gun'. What does this suggest about her attitude to the game?

d) How does the writer describe Steffi's opponent, Gaby, when she is losing?

e) Who won the match that is being described?

f) What happens to these two players at the next tournament in which they play?

2 Use these tasks and questions to help you interpret the text.
  a) Does the writer like or dislike Steffi Graf? How can you tell?
  b) Which of these statements about the article do you agree/disagree with?
    A Steffi Graf seems very determined.
    B She seems very talented.
    C She seems very cold.
    D She seems very emotional.
    E She is very upset to lose her match.
    F She makes mistakes but quickly learns from them.

  c) For each statement (A–F) that you agree with, write down a quotation from the text to prove it is true.
  d) Find a sentence that:
     i) is description
     ii) is dialogue
     iii) refers to the author and audience.
  e) The article is written in two paragraphs. Write a sentence that summarises the content of each paragraph.

3 What is the purpose of this writing?
  ● To inform
  ● To entertain
  ● To persuade
  ● Something else?
  Explain how you know, using examples from the text.

4 Did you enjoy the article? Say what you like or dislike about it.

Activity 3 Writing sports journalism

Choose one of the topics below (A or B) and write the opening sentence of a sports article. Spend time getting the opening sentence right. Then write the first part of the article, aiming to entertain and inform your reader.
A Introduce your reader to a sport that you like – e.g. netball, skateboarding, Frisbee.
B Write a match report on a game/match you have recently watched or played in.

Assess your progress

Underline or highlight examples of the following in your sports article that you think are successful:
● writing that entertains
● writing that informs
● some description
● some dialogue
● carefully chosen language that shows your opinion.

Assessment task

A well-known and very popular electrical product has developed a major fault. An entire batch of this product has been sold and, within days, has malfunctioned in a large number of homes. Several people around the country have been injured as a result.

Write a newspaper article about this to go on the front page of a national daily newspaper. Follow these steps to help you plan and write your article.

1 Decide which electrical product you will choose to be the subject of your article – and the fault which it has developed.

4 Decide what to put in each paragraph of your article. Refer back to the work you did on structuring a news story (Section 2) to make sure you think of everything you need.
Remember to plan where you will use your quotes from the public, the manufacturer and reviews of the product.

2 As a journalist, you will need to interview people who have been injured and, perhaps, their families. Write down some of the quotes you might want to use in your article. You may also want to interview someone from the company that manufactures the electrical product. Write down what they might say.

DAILY NEWS

5 Write a headline for your story. Check back on the work you did in Section 1 to help you.

6 Write the news story.

7 Make sure you are happy with the structure of your news story. Did you stick to your plan?

3 You may want to refer to some of the reviews written about this product when it was first produced. Write some positive and negative comments about the product that could have appeared in these reviews.

8 Make sure your story is well spelt, well punctuated and makes good sense.

Non-fiction is usually found in books rather than in, say, leaflets or pamphlets. It includes:

- autobiography
- biography
- speeches
- travel writing
- reportage.

You will learn:

- how to write effectively about yourself
- how to write interestingly about another person
- how to describe people and places in an entertaining way
- how to write a powerfully persuasive speech.

2 Literary non-fiction

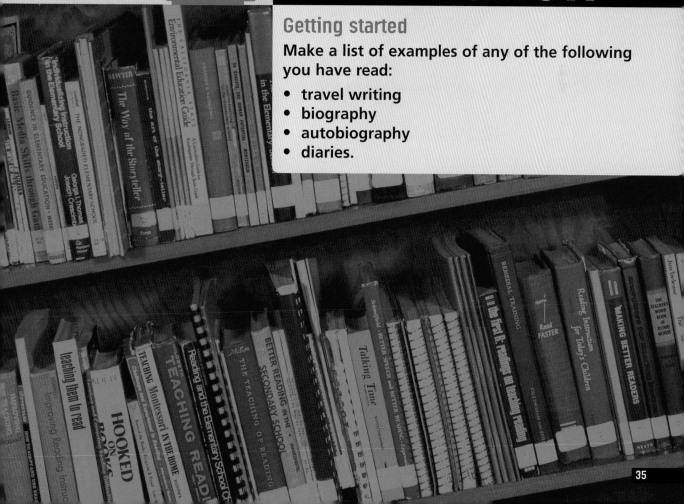

Getting started

Make a list of examples of any of the following you have read:

- travel writing
- biography
- autobiography
- diaries.

1

Looking at autobiography

You will learn:

- how different writers describe their own lives
- different ways of writing an autobiography.

Autobiographies are texts that we write about ourselves. They tell our life story. Sometimes these are written towards the end of someone's life (looking back on what they have achieved). Sometimes, younger celebrities (e.g. Wayne Rooney or Jordan) write them.

Activity 1 Thinking about autobiographies

Look at the two opinions below. Which do you agree with? Use a writing frame like the one below to explain your own point of view.

Opinion A

I think it's mad that someone who's in their early 20s can write an autobiography. What do they have to write about? They haven't lived. It's just another example of how people want to read about celebrities all the time.

Opinion B

If people want to read about celebrities, then why not let them write their autobiographies? Their lives might be really interesting even though they've still got a long time ahead of them.

My opinion

I agree with opinion _____ . I agree with her comment that '_____'

because _____ . A good example of this is _____

because _____ .

Activity 2 Starting an autobiography

Many autobiographies start at the beginning of the writer's life: 'I was born in …' But they can also start in less predictable ways.

1 Use a spider diagram to brainstorm about six other ways that a writer could begin an autobiography.

2 The next page gives examples of different openings for an autobiography. The writer has been advised to try to grab the reader's attention from the start. Put these openings in order of best to worst.

Opening A

I was born in Stafford in 1962. Stafford is not a place that many people know much about. It's a bit quiet, a bit safe, even (put your hands over your eyes people of Stafford) a bit dull.

Opening B

I'll skip being born and all that because I know you're not interested. So life for me begins aged ten on the see-saw at the playing fields of Yelverton Avenue, just a few hundred yards away from my house but to be honest a world away.

Opening C

I was born at 11 Yelverton Avenue Stafford on 27 October 1962 and lived there until I was eighteen, when I moved away from home to go to university at Lancaster.

Opening D

My mother had thought she'd finished having babies. She'd had Jean and Michael, my brother and sister, and in her mid-40s went to the doctor with what she thought was a heavy cold. She was in for a terrible surprise.

Opening E

I liked my childhood. I had a nice home, good friends and a caring family. I had a cat (Thomas, a girl, but we didn't know that when we got her), two guinea pigs and possibly some goldfish, though I can't remember much about them. And the guinea pigs ate each other so I've tried to forget about them too.

3 Choose the opening you like best. Write a paragraph saying what you like about it. Try to say something about:
   - the content (what it's about)
   - the style (how it is written)
   - the vocabulary (the words the writer uses)
   - the sentences (whether they are long, short, simple, complex).

4 Choose the opening you like least. How do you think it could be improved? Write a paragraph as if you were the writer's teacher explaining how the text could be improved.

Activity 3 Reading *Toast*

In his 2003 autobiography *Toast*, Nigel Slater lets readers learn about his life through his memories of food. Read the start of his book. Then complete the tasks and questions to help you explore the text.

My mother is scraping a piece of burned toast out of the kitchen window, a crease of annoyance across her forehead. This is not an occasional occurrence, a once-in-a-while hiccup in a busy mother's day. My mother burns the toast as surely as the sun rises each morning. In fact, I doubt if she has ever made a round of toast in her life that failed to fill the kitchen with plumes of throat-catching smoke. I am nine now and have never seen the butter without black bits in it.

1   What do you think Nigel Slater means by 'a crease of annoyance' on his mother's forehead?

2   Choose a word or phrase which shows that Nigel Slater's mother regularly burns the toast.

3   What do you think he means by 'throat-catching smoke'?

4   What are the 'black bits' in the butter?

5   Re-read the opening sentence of the extract. How does it try to grab your attention and make you want to read on? Think about:

a) the picture it creates in your mind

b) any questions it makes you ask.

6   List three other examples of how Nigel Slater tries to make someone burning toast interesting to read about.

7   Which of these words best describes the way Nigel Slater writes in the extract? Choose the most suitable word, then write a sentence to explain your choice.

happy	unhappy
nostalgic	descriptive
affectionate	detailed
warm	sensuous (using the different senses a lot)
aggressive	memorable

Activity 4   Writing an autobiography

Choose a key moment from your own childhood – perhaps a birthday or other celebration, a family occasion, getting into trouble. Write the opening of your autobiography which brings your memory to life. Aim to:

- have an opening sentence that grabs your reader's attention
- use vivid language to paint a picture of the scene
- use a variety of sentences.

Assess your progress

Pick one example from your writing which shows how you have achieved each of the bullet points in Activity 4. Write a sentence or two for each, explaining how they achieve what you were aiming for.

2

Comparing autobiographies

You will learn:
- how to compare the language of two texts
- how writers write about their childhood.

Below are two extracts from autobiographies in which the writers look at their childhood. One takes place around 1900; the other nearer the end of the twentieth century.

Activity 1 Reading the texts

Skimming is a useful skill for getting the gist of a text. It means reading a text quickly to gain a general idea of what it is about. Read Texts A and B to get the gist of each one.

Text A

Babies were not welcomed in our family. I have heard my mother say on more than one occasion in her middle age that if she had to live her life again and knew as much as she did, then she wouldn't have had one of us. She told me she even took gunpowder to get rid of *me*, mixing it to a paste in a soapdish on her washstand every night. I hope she didn't hold it against me that I refused to budge. When I was born, the doctor called me a very strong healthy child, so much so that he used *me* to vaccinate six other children from. This seems horrifying nowadays but it was the usual thing then, to take serum from one child to another. Mother even knew the names of some of the six who went to school with me.

Well as I have said, none of us had an enthusiastic welcome. I can never remember in all my life being cuddled or kissed or 'loved' as we love our babies today. I think all this gave me an inferiority complex which has lasted all my life. Even today I feel most unwilling to enter a room full of people. I always feel I have no right to be there, and if everyone turns to look at me I wish I could drop through the floor.

Text B

My family are the most important people in my life. I love them all to bits. Through the bad times and the good times they have always been there for me, especially my mum. It is something the press has managed to twist over the years. The way some journalists have described my background, you would think I had the most miserable and unstable childhood, which couldn't be further from the truth. Yes, my real dad finally walked out on the family when I was three, but I had hardly seen him anyway, so he was no loss to me. After that, my mum fell in love with Paul Price and, although I've never called him Dad, I definitely see him in that role. He and Mum got married when I was nine and they have the strongest marriage of anyone I know.

1 Which of these sentences best sums up the gist of Text A?
  A The writer had a nasty childhood.
  B The writer had a cruel mother.
  C The writer was unwanted and has never recovered.
  D The writer continues to feel unloved many years after she was born.
  E Life was different in 1900.

2 Write a sentence explaining your choice. Why do you think it best sums up the text?

3 How would you summarise Text A in one sentence?

4 Which of these sentences best sums up Text B?
  A The writer had a happy childhood.
  B The media often tell lies.
  C The writer's family mean everything to her.
  D Although she's had a tough time, her family have always been there for her
  E People don't really understand the writer.

5 Write a sentence explaining your choice. Why do you think it best sums up the text?

6 How would you summarise Text B in one sentence?

Activity 2 Comparing two texts

Look back at Texts A and B in Activity 1.

1 List three things you think these texts have in common.

2 List four things that make the texts different.

3 List three clues that tell you which of the two texts is older and which is newer.

4 In one sentence, say which text you prefer and why.

Activity 3 Being an editor

Text A in Activity 1 is by Faith Dorothy Osberby, who was aged ten in 1900.

Imagine you are a newspaper editor. You are about to print this extract to tie in with the publication of her autobiography. Decide on:
● the title you would give the article
● the image you would use to encourage readers to read the extract
● the introductory paragraph you would write to explain to readers what the text is about.

Assess your progress

Write a sentence or two about each of your decisions above. Explain what effect you wanted to achieve and how you have tried to achieve it.

3

Looking at biographies

You will learn:

- how writers make other people's lives come to life on the page.

'Bio' means 'life' and 'graph' means 'writing', so biographies tell the stories of other people's lives. They way they do this varies.

Activity 1 Thinking about biographies

Imagine you have been asked to write the biography of a famous person or hero. Your publisher has asked you to think of someone:

- who interests or intrigues you
- who has influenced you positively
- whose life you think would be interesting to other people.

1 Who would you choose as the subject of your biography? Explain why you made this choice.

2 What are the main things you would like to describe about this person's life (e.g. key moments of triumph or sadness, difficulties they overcame, successes)?

3 Think of a good opening sentence for your biography.

Activity 2 Exploring facts and description

A biography can be a purely factual text, giving nothing but the essential facts about a person's life.

1. Take a look at this brief biography of William Shakespeare, which appears in an encyclopaedia of people's lives. Then answer the questions to help you understand the text.

Shakespeare, William (1564–1616)

English dramatist and poet. Established in London by 1589 as an actor and dramatist, he is considered the greatest English dramatist. Born in Stratford-on-Avon, the son of a wool dealer, he was educated at the grammar school and, in 1582, married Anne Hathaway. They had a daughter, Susanna (1583) and twins Hamnet (died 1596) and Judith (1595).

a) What did Shakespeare's father do?

b) Who was Shakespeare's wife?

c) How many children did the couple have?

d) What happened to Shakespeare's son, Hamnet?

e) To what age did Shakespeare live?

2. Choose someone sitting in your class, or a parent/carer, or use yourself as a subject. Write a paragraph about this person that is purely factual. Make it a short, factual account that could appear in an encyclopaedia of biography. It might include:
   - the person's date of birth
   - the names of their parents
   - key events in their life.

Activity 3 Comparing factual and descriptive writing in biography

The biographer and novelist Peter Ackroyd recently wrote a biography of William Shakespeare. It is about 500 pages long. Look at the way he describes Shakespeare's birth. Use the tasks below to help you explore the text.

The infant Shakespeare was carried by his father from his birthplace in Henley Street down the High Street and Church Street into the church itself. The mother was never present at the baptism. John Shakespeare and his newborn son would have been accompanied by the godparents, who were otherwise known as the 'god-sips' or 'gossips'. On this occasion the godfather was William Smith, a haberdasher and neighbour in Henley Street. The name of the infant was given before he was dipped in the **font** and the sign of the cross marked upon his forehead. At the font the gossips were **exhorted** to make sure that William Shakespeare heard sermons and learned the **creed** as well as the Lord's Prayer 'in the English tongue'. After the baptism a piece of white linen cloth was placed on the head of the child, and remained there until the mother had been 'churched' or purified; it was called the 'chrisom cloth' and, if the Infant died within a month, was used as a shroud … In the sixteenth century, the mortality of the newly born was high. Nine per cent died within a week of birth, and a further 11 per cent before they were a month old; in the decade of Shakespeare's own birth there were in Stratford 62.8 average annual baptisms and 42.8 average annual child burials. You had to be tough, or from a relatively prosperous family, to survive the odds. It is likely that Shakespeare had both of these advantages.

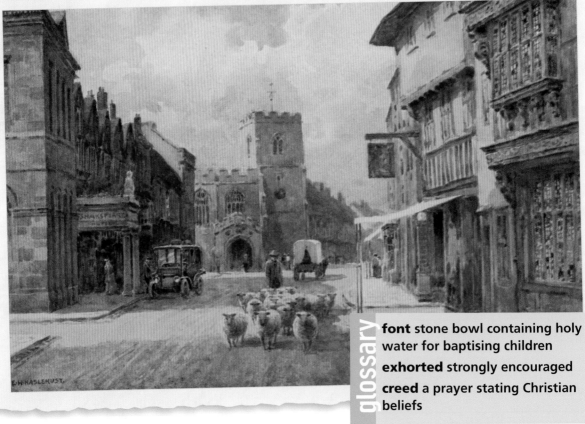

glossary

font stone bowl containing holy water for baptising children

exhorted strongly encouraged

creed a prayer stating Christian beliefs

1 List two similarities between this text and the text in Activity 2.

2 List three differences between the two texts.

3 Write down one piece of information under each of these headings to show what you have learnt from the text in Activity 3.
- What we learn about Stratford.
- What we learn about Shakespeare's godparents.
- What we learn about language.
- What we learn about life in the sixteenth century.
- What we learn about traditions and customs.

4 Obviously, Peter Ackroyd was born long after Shakespeare died. How is he able to write about an event that took place over four hundred years ago?

5 How do you think readers of the texts in Activities 2 and 3 would differ? What might readers be looking for in the biography that they wouldn't find in the encyclopaedia? You might structure your answer like this:

> I would be reading the biography text with some different purposes. These would include: ...

Activity 4 Researching a biography

Choose someone at school or at home – another student, a friend, a member of your family or family friend, and think about how you would research or write their biography.

1 Ask them questions about their earliest years, such as:
- where and when they were born
- what they know about the place (the town, the hospital)
- what life was like then (what music was popular, how technology was different)
- how the birth went
- whether they were part of a ceremony, as Shakespeare was.

2 Now write the opening page of a biography of this person. Aim to capture the flavour of the period in the same way that Peter Ackroyd does in Activity 3. Try to create a vivid picture of:
- your subject
- their memories
- what life was like when they were born.

Assess your progress

Ask the subject of your biography to read your writing and comment on its effectiveness. You could ask them to write down their answers to the following questions.
- Does the biography match your memories of this time?
- Which details are most effective in creating a picture of that time?
- Which words are most effective in creating that picture?
- What details or words would make this biography even more effective?

4

Exploring newspaper biographies

You will learn:

- how to structure a biography of someone in just 500 words.

A biography isn't always published in book form. When famous people die, for example, newspapers sometimes publish articles that tell the whole life story in 500 to 1000 words. These are called obituaries. Many newspapers also run 'profiles' of people in the news, giving us more information about their background and beliefs.

Writing a short biography is very different from writing a book about someone's life.

Activity 1 Exploring the text-type

Imagine someone famous has died. A newspaper wishes to publish a 500-word summary of their life. Use the questions below to think about how you might approach the task.

1 What sources of information might you use to research the celebrity?

2 How will you condense 60 or more years of someone's life into just 500 words? Will you try to say something about every stage of their life? Or will you focus on a few main achievements?

5 What style should you use? Should it be impersonal (where you focus on the celebrity without giving your own opinions)? Or should it be personal (allowing you to say things like 'I think …' and 'I believe …')?

3 How would you start your biography? With facts about when the person was born (or is that too predictable and boring)? How else might you start?

4 What tone would you use? Should the profile only say positive things about the celebrity (bearing in mind they have recently died)? Or should it be an honest, warts-and-all account?

Activity 2 Reading a profile

Some newspaper profiles sum up a person's special skills or achievements without describing their whole life. Read this profile of surfer Duncan Scott. Look at how the writer informs us about his life in just a few lines. Then use the tasks and questions to help you understand and interpret the text.

'What most people see when they surf in Cornwall is what happens at the height of summer, when the waves are pretty small,' explains 28 year-old Duncan Scott. 'The

5 average punter's surfing experience is going down to the beach with a bucket and spade, with the waves lapping at your ankles. But winter changes that round, to say the least.'

Down a phone line from his home

10 in Newquay, South Africa-born Scott – a professional surfer for eight years – is excitedly talking me through the spine-tingling fun he had on Monday, when he and three other surf addicts rode waves that

15 reached their peak at the Cribbar reef, off Fistral beach. Comparing pictures taken that day with archive photographs, he says, suggests that they now have a justified claim – cue garlands, Beach Boys songs and a

20 place in the Guinness Book of Records – to having tackled the biggest waves ever surfed in the UK: 40ft swells that measure up handsomely to the ones he has surfed in Hawaii and northern California.

25 Via such websites as buoyweather.com and magicseaweed.com, Scott, Daniel Joel, Sam Lamiroy and Llewelyn Whittaker had been following the progress of a storm that was scheduled to send waves into the

30 Cornish coast early this week. 'The colour coding moves from yellow, through green to yellow, to orange, to kind of brain-tumour red,' he explains, with no little enthusiasm. 'And with a few days to go, we were getting

35 a lot of brain-tumour red.'

These things often turn out to be anticlimaxes, but this time the weather – which has to be mild with a gentle wind, so as not to break the waves up – was spot on. 'I couldn't sleep the previous night, I 40 was so wound up,' says Scott. 'At about 7 a.m. I loaded up on coffee and went to Truro to get my jetski.' Fielding repeated calls on his mobile while trying to fill the jetski with petrol, Scott so forgot himself 45 that he mislaid his wallet en route. The quartet finally made it to the beach in the early afternoon.

'The worst-case scenarios are breaking bones, or smashing up your board, or 50 getting run over by the jetski,' he explains, with all the level-headedness of someone giving gardening advice. 'But the main risk is drowning. If you get dragged down, it's not like holding your head underwater and 55 not being able to breathe. It feels like being kicked in by a couple of hoodlums. And obviously, the bigger the wave, the bigger the risk.'

That day, mercifully, everything went 60 according to plan. 'It's not like hitting a good golf shot or scoring a goal in soccer,' he explains. 'For the time that you're riding the wave and then dropping down, it's like freefalling out of a plane – just absolutely 65 amazing. And then you surface and it's like, "Wow! Incredible! I didn't drown!" The adrenaline rush is quite something: you fly on that right into the evening. But there's a big comedown. You get headaches.' 70

And the duration of the experience? 'About 12 seconds,' he says. 'But it's worth it.'

1 Using a spider diagram, write down what facts we learn about Duncan Scott – for example, his age, where he lives, what his job is, how long he has been doing it and so on.

2 Answer these questions to help you understand some more of the facts given in the profile.

a) What do surfers use websites for?

b) What does a storm colour-coded red mean?

c) What two examples show how excited Scott was about his day of surfing?

d) What is the worst thing that can happen when you are surfing?

3 Scott describes what happens after surfing the wave. In your own words, write down three of these things.

4 The profile focuses on the events of one or two days, but it also tells us quite a lot about Scott. To help with your interpretation, write down two words or phrases that describe different aspects of his character. For each one, give evidence from the text that supports your opinion.

5 Give each paragraph in the profile a subheading that sums up what the paragraph is about.

6 Write down why you think the writer chose to begin the article with a quotation from Duncan Scott.

7 Find examples of the way John Harris does these things in his article.

A John Harris shows that he admires Duncan Scott.

B The writer uses an informal word rather than writing more formally.

C The writer gives facts and figures.

D The writer packs a lot of information into a sentence.

E The writer describes Scott's emotions.

F The writer uses dialogue.

G The writer uses dramatic language.

H The writer uses connectives to link ideas.

I As well as statements and descriptions, the writer also uses a question.

8 Choose three of the examples above (A–I) and write a sentence or two for each, explaining the effect they have.

9 What is the purpose of this text? Choose from the list below. You may decide it is a mixture of two or more things. For each purpose you identify, write a sentence to show how the article achieves this purpose.

- To inform
- To describe
- To persuade
- To explain
- To entertain

10 Which audience is this text aimed at? Think about age and gender. Is it for an audience with specific interests or a more general audience?

11 What would be a more boring way of writing this profile? Think up a couple of boring opening sentences, then write one or two sentences explaining what makes it boring.

Activity 3   Writing a profile

Think of someone you know, then focus on a particular experience that means a lot to them – e.g. passing a test or exam, getting a qualification, learning a new skill, surviving an awful experience.

1 Write a 500-word profile that focuses on the skill or experience and, in the process, tells us about the person. Your teacher will give you a template to help you plan and write your profile. Before you begin writing:
- decide on the audience your text will be aimed at
- decide on the purpose(s) you want your writing to achieve.

Note down the features you will use in your writing to achieve both of these.

2 Using a list or a spider diagram, decide on the key point you will make in each paragraph.
- Number these points in the best order.
- Then decide what you are going to tell us about this person as you write about their experience. Write these facts next to the key point of the paragraph in which you will include this information.

Use the example below to help you.

Audience – teenagers – mixture of formal and informal language; some slang	
Purpose – to entertain and inform	
Inform:	facts about Hayley; age; where she lives; how long been dancing; other exams taken
Describe:	Hayley's feelings; the exam room

age, how long dancing, where Hayley lives

describe Hayley's feelings

3. Quote: what Hayley thinks about the exam

1. Quote: what Hayley thinks about dancing

2. The night before the exam

Hayley's dance exam

6. After the exam

quote: Hayley's feelings

5. The exam

describe Hayley's feelings; exam room

4. The morning before the exam – other exams taken before

Assess your progress

Look back to the points in Task 7, Activity 2 (page 48). Which of these features can you identify in your own writing? Use arrows and labels to highlight where you have used them. Choose three that you have not used and try to add them into your writing.

5

Looking at travel writing

You will learn:

• more about travel writing

• how to write vivid descriptions of experiences and places.

Travel writing is another type of literary non-fiction. It is a popular choice in bookshops with books devoted to describing people's journeys and adventures to unfamiliar places.

Activity 1 Reading travel writing

Dervla Murphy is a famous Irish traveller who often travels by bike or on horseback through places like Asia and Ethiopia. In this extract she is on the Turkish/Iranian frontier. Read it, then use the tasks and questions to help you explore the text.

At Dogubayzit, the last little town en route to the Persian frontier-post, I stayed in the local doss-house, where my bedroom was a tiny box leading off the wide loft which accommodated the majority of the hotel's patrons. This room had a flimsy door, without any fastening, and there was no movable piece of furniture which could have been placed against it as a security measure. The squalid bedding was inhabited by a host of energetic fleas, but their attentions were wasted on me and within minutes of retiring I was sound asleep.

1 Dervla Murphy describes the place where she stays as a 'doss-house' and a 'hotel'.

   a) What makes it seem like a doss-house (a cheap lodging house for example used by tramps)?

   b) What makes it seem like a hotel?

   c) Why does Murphy look for a movable piece of furniture in her tiny room?

   d) What other ways might the writer might have said 'the squalid bedding was inhabited by a host of energetic fleas'?

2 Which of these words do you think best describes Murphy? Write a sentence to explain your choice. Explain why you have chosen one word rather than another with a similar meaning.

brave	inquisitive
reckless	worried
adventurous	insecure
curious	fascinated
tough	foolhardy
intrepid	

3 Why might a reader be interested in reading about Dervla Murphy's experience in this hotel?

Activity 2 Exploring descriptive writing

Some of the earliest travel writing was by explorers and adventurers who were discovering new lands and new species of animals. Their books described what they saw. As a result, travel writing often uses lots of description.

Look at the example on the next page written by Cecil Gosling in the early twentieth century. Working and travelling in Paraguay, South America, he describes an encounter with a piranha fish.

Perhaps the most dangerous inhabitant of the Paraguayan waters is the piranha, which I suspect of causing more loss of life to man and beast than alligators, surubis or mangarajus, and such like aquatic monsters. The piranha is a scaled fish, similar in shape to our European perch, only the head is of more aggressive appearance, the mouth being armed with a most formidable set of teeth, more like those of a wild animal than a fish. With these, and aided by his powerful jaws, there is literally nothing that he will not bite through. I have put a lead pencil into the mouth of one, and seen it bitten clean off, and I have also seen him bite off the edge of a keenly tempered knife. His ferocity is equally developed, and one has to be very careful in handling these demons when caught, and when getting the hooks out of their mouths. When taken out of the water they make a barking noise.

A friend of mine, a police inspector, while bathing, was attacked by a shoal of them, which mutilated him in such a manner that he at once swam back to the bank to the spot where his clothes were, picked up his revolver and blew his brains out.

1 This text – like a lot of travel writing – gives a lot of descriptive detail. In this case it is about a creature rather than a place. Using the detail in the first paragraph, draw a rough sketch of a piranha fish, labelling it with the key information about its appearance, behaviour and sound.

2 Make a note underneath your sketch of any information that would have made it more accurate but was not in the text (e.g. the shape or size of a piranha). Why do you think the writer left these details out?

3 Find three words that help you to visualise the piranha, to imagine what it looks like.

4 Look at these statements about the text. For each one, say whether you think it is true (T), false (F) or there is not enough evidence (NEE). Then, alongside your choice, give an example of a word or phrase from the text that supports your opinion.

A The writer dislikes piranha fish.
B Piranha fish are silver.
C Getting hooks out of their mouths is easy enough.
D In some ways piranhas are not like fish.
E The writer uses some complicated words.
F The writer tells us about himself as well as about the piranha.
G He writes in a very cold, heartless way about the incident with the police inspector.

5 Some readers might think this text doesn't feel like travel writing. Using Dervla Murphy's text for comparison, give two reasons that suggest it *is* travel writing and two reasons that suggest it is a *different* text-type.

Activity 3 Exploring the text-type

It seems obvious that travel writing is writing about someone's travels! Use this activity to explore it more by thinking how it is different from other text-types. Fill in the gaps in this paragraph to develop your thinking.

Travel writing may feel similar to autobiographical writing because (a) _____ . It will be different from travel brochures and travel websites because their aim is to (b) _____ , whereas the aim of travel writing is to (c) _____ . I would expect the language of travel writing to include (d) _____ . I think people will read travel writing because they are interested in (e) _____ . Travel writing can help us to learn more about other people and cultures. This is important because (f) _____ .

Activity 4 Exploring detailed descriptive writing

1 Practise your own skills in detailed descriptive writing. Choose a place, creature or object that you can look at. Make notes on its details, paying attention to the different senses (how it looks, sounds, smells and so on). You could choose:
   - a pet
   - a place you know (your bedroom, kitchen, particular seat and desk in school)
   - another environment (e.g. fish-tank, rabbit hutch).

2 Now, as vividly as you can, write a detailed descriptive passage about your chosen topic.

Assess your progress

Re-write tasks 1–3 in Activity 2 so that they apply to your writing. Then ask a partner to answer them. Use their answers to improve your writing.

6

Examining a longer travel writing text

You will learn:

- how writers structure longer texts
- how to use different techniques to hold your reader's interest.

Travel writers often enjoy describing the more unpleasant experiences they have on their journeys, such as terrible accommodation, and menacing people and creatures.

Activity 1 Examining a longer text

In his book *Hunting Mr Heartbreak*, Jonathan Raban describes his journey across America. On his travels, he stays in a rented summer house in one of the hot southern states. Read what happens, then explore the language and structure of the text. The questions around the text are designed to help you get the gist, or overview. The questions at the end are designed to help you explore specific points.

1 How does the writer make the ants seem both harmless and menacing? Pick out a word or phrase for each.

2 How does the writer show us the way William the pharmacist speaks?

3 What do you make of the 'twinkle' in William as he talks about the fire ants?

It took me a while to notice the ants. Unpacking my sponge bag in the bathroom, I thought I saw the brown shagpile carpet ripple like a cornfield in a wind. Looking closer I saw a colony of ants
5   the size of wasps out on some kind of jungle exercise in the woolly undergrowth. When I flushed the cistern, a hundred or so ant-marines tumbled into the toilet bowl from their positions under the rim.
10   I drove the Spirit back into town, a mile away, and consulted my new friend William, the pharmacist. 'They black ants? Or are they a kind of reddy-brown?'
      'Black – I think.'
15   'I hope it's black ants you got out there; if they're a brown ant, it could be you got fire ants on your place. Then you got problems.' He was searching round among his poisons.
      'Friend of mine, he had fire ants once . . . he
20   just went out into his back yard one morning . . . end of the day, his daughter came home, found him laying there dayud. Yes – he was killed by the fire ants,' he said with the same soft twinkle that he'd used to speak of tornados. 'That was a
25   misfortunate man.'
      As he spoke, my ants started changing colour rapidly from black to brown.
      'But if they're inside your house, they'll most likely be black ants. I hope so, anyway. I wouldn't
30   like to think of you with fire ants in your house.

How big you say they are?'
      I found it hard to control the trembling of my forefinger and thumb.
      William nodded and smiled; he looked significantly pleased by what I'd shown him.   35
      'Oh, yes, we do get them real big around here –'
      [. . .]
      Back at the cabin, I moved as cautiously as if I was burgling it, examining each patch of carpet before I dared plant a foot there. But there was   40
no question: my ants were coal-black; not deadly, just a nuisance to be got rid of. Following the instructions on the bottle, I booby-trapped the house with half-inch rectangles of white card, then shook on each card a couple of drops of   45
the poisonous clear syrup. Within a quarter of an hour, the ants were assembled around the cards like so many guests at an all-male black-tie dinner. I watched over them with an odd hostly feeling of benevolence. Poisoners, I remembered, tend to   50
have milk-and-water manners – like Dr Crippen, described by the sea captain who was responsible for his arrest as 'the acme of politeness'.
      As they rose from their banquet to return to headquarters, the ants blundered away from table,   55
limped, staggered, fell to their knees. Their legs kept on waving feebly long after their thoraxes had hit the deck. Quietly cheered by the slaughter, I poured myself a finger of Scotch and went out to sit in my rocker on the porch and admire the scenery.   60

4 How can you tell that the writer is getting nervous?

5 Which words does the writer use which make the ants seem as if they have human qualities?

6 What impression of the writer do you get from the text? Choose a word from below that best sums him up. Then write a sentence to explain your choice.
- nervous
- adventurous
- wise
- foolhardy
- curious
- aggressive
- funny
- confused

7 One way the writer makes the picture of the ants especially vivid is through comparison. For example, he compares ants to wasps to create the impression that the ants are more vicious and threatening.

Now describe the effects of the comparisons below. If you think the comparison is designed to make the ants seem funny or harmless, draw a smiley face. If you think it makes the ants seem threatening or dangerous, draw a frowning face.

Comparison	What effect does this create?	Do ants seem threatening or harmless?
'I saw the brown shagpile carpet ripple like a cornfield in a wind'		
'on some kind of jungle exercise'		
'a hundred or so ant-marines'		
'ants were assembled around the cards like so many guests at an all-male black-tie dinner'		

8 What is the writer's intended effect on the reader when he makes the ants seem:

a) harmless   b) threatening?

Assess your progress

For each sentence below, tick the box you feel applies to your understanding.

	Er … no, not really	I think so	I'm sure of it
I understand what the text is about.			
I can say where in the text the writer tries to entertain or frighten the reader.			
I can comment on how the writer's choice of language makes the text entertaining or frightening.			
I have a strong impression of the writer's personality.			
I can comment on how the text shows the writer's personality.			

7

Looking at diaries

You will learn:
- how language is used in diaries.

Many people keep diaries to record their thoughts and feelings. Sometimes these are in the form of on-line blogs; sometimes they are in the form of notebooks.

Activity 1 Exploring the text–type

1 Throughout history, people have kept diaries. Why do you think this is? Look at the suggestions below. Then put them in order of most important to least important reason.

People keep a diary because …
A It helps us to look back over our lives.
B It makes us feel important.
C It enables us to share our thoughts and feelings with other people.
D It enables us to sort out our inner feelings by writing them down.
E It is a way of dealing with difficult issues.
F It helps us to look back and understand difficult patches in our lives.
G It gives us time to think about and explain experiences long after they have happened.

2 If diaries are for recording personal experiences, why are they published as books and why do other people like to read them? Which do you think is the main reason?
A We are basically nosey.
B We like to learn about other people, other places and other periods of time.
C They help us to learn about other people.
D We might learn that our own problems aren't perhaps as serious as we might have thought – it puts our lives into perspective.

Activity 2 Reading diaries

There are several examples of published diaries such as those by:
- Samuel Pepys, written in the seventeenth century
- poets and novelists
- people who work for the royal family
- people in prison.

Here are two diary extracts that describe the experiences of people in terrible situations.

The first, written in 1912, is an extract from Captain Scott's diary towards the end of his expedition to the South Pole in which he and his four companions would die.

The second is a diary entry by Sarah Macnaughton, who helped the Red Cross with those injured during the First World War.

Use the questions that follow to explore these texts.

Saturday 17 March

I can only write at lunch and then only occasionally. The cold is intense – minus 40° at midday. My companions are unendingly cheerful, but we are all on the verge of serious frostbites, and though we constantly talk of fetching through I don't think anyone of us believes it in his heart. We march now, and at all times except meals. Yesterday we had to lay up for a blizzard and today we move dreadfully slowly. We are at No. 14 pony camp, only two pony marches from One Ton Depot. We leave here our theodolite, a camera and Oates's sleeping-bags. Diaries, etc., and geological specimens carried at Wilson's special request, will be found with us or on our sledge.

Sunday 18 March

Today, lunch, we are 21 miles from the depot. Ill fortune presses, but better may come. We have had more wind and drift from ahead yesterday; had to stop marching; wind NW, force 4, temp. minus 35 . No human being could face it, and we are worn out, *nearly*. My right foot has gone – two days ago I was the proud possessor of best feet. They are the steps of my downfall.

Text A: Captain Scott

22 September 1914

At midnight the first shell came over us with a shriek. I went down and woke the orderlies and doctors. We dressed and went over to help move the wounded at the hospital. The shells began to scream overhead. It was a bright moonlit night, and we walked without haste — a small body of women — across the road to the hospital. Here we found the wounded all yelling like mad things, thinking they were going to be left behind.

Nearly all the moving to the cellars had already been done — only three stretchers remained to be moved. One wounded English sergeant helped us. We sat in the cellars, with one night-light burning in each, and with 70 wounded men to take care of. Two of them were dying. There was only one line of bricks between us and the shells. One shell fell into the garden, making a hole six feet deep; the next crashed through a house on the opposite side of the road and set it on fire.

We stayed there all night.

Text B: Sarah Macnaughton

1 Read Text A, then answer these questions.
  a) Why was it difficult for Captain Scott to write very often?
  b) Why did the explorers have to stop marching?
  c) What do you understand by 'geological specimens'?

2 Now read Text B and answer these questions.
  a) Why do you think patients had been moved to the cellars?
  b) How many wounded men were there to take care of?
  c) Why do you think the wounded and medical staff stayed in the cellars all night?

3   To help you interpret these texts, use a table like the one below to note down what they tell us about Captain Scott and Sarah Macnaughton. Then answer the questions underneath.

	Captain Scott	Sarah Macnaughton
The character of the writer		
The conditions in which they are living		
How hopeful or optimistic they are		

a) What three things do the two diaries have in common?

b) What three things make them seem different?

c) Apart from the use of dates, what clues are there in the language that these are diary entries rather than letters or stories?

4   Think about which text grabs your attention more. Does it do this because of what the writer is saying? Or is because of how they write it?

5   Think about what makes people want to read diaries. What do you think is the most important thing?

Activity 3   Writing a diary

Keep a diary for one week. At the end of each day, try to spend about five minutes writing it. You don't need to record anything important – just your thoughts and reflections on things that happen to you and how they make you feel. You might make a note of conversations you overhear, jokes, funny things you read and so on.

Your starting point could be the day you have had so far – beginning with waking up this morning.

Assess your progress

1   Write down three things that you think a reader of your diary could tell about your personality and your life.

2   Ask a partner to read your diary and do the same. Compare your points. Do you agree? Work together to identify evidence in the text to support your points.

3   Still working with your partner, write a sentence or two in which you explain how effectively you think your diary tells the reader about you and your life.

8

Exploring speeches

You will learn:
• what makes a
  good speech.

Speeches are often used to persuade, inform or entertain people. They are an important part of the way decisions are made. From the Houses of Parliament to the United Nations, people use speeches to try to get their ideas across. Think of aircraft announcements, where a member of the cabin crew uses a speech to inform us about safety procedures. Think of stand-up comedians who use speeches to entertain us and make us laugh.

Activity 1 Exploring the purposes of speeches

Look at the list of speeches in the table on page 61. For each one, decide:
• its purpose
• another way in which the same message might be communicated
• whether you think a speech is the best way of communicating the message.

Use the table to help you note your responses.

Speech	Possible purpose	One other way of communicating the message	Is a speech the best way of communicating the message?
1 A school assembly 2 A speech in Parliament 3 A sports coach to a team before an important game 4 A local politician addressing an audience 5 The Education Minister addressing teachers at a conference	e.g. a) To change someone's mind about a topic b) To get someone to do things differently c) To educate people about something d) To make people laugh e) To change someone's mood	e.g. poster leaflet podcast article one-to-one conversation letter	☐ Yes ☐ No

Activity 2 Exploring the features of speeches

In your time at school you will have experienced hundreds of speeches, mainly in school assemblies. Think about the ingredients of a good and bad speech.

1 Imagine you are the coach of a school team – e.g. rounders, dodgeball, debating, table tennis. Give a team pep-talk before their next game. Your talk should motivate the team after a really bad defeat in their last game.

2 Now write an example of how *not* to make such a speech.

a) Write the opening one or two paragraphs.

b) Use labels and arrows to explain what makes your speech bad. Try to say something about the following.

- Purpose: does it completely fail to do what it should?
- Content (what is in the speech): are all the important details missing?
- Language: is it far too formal or far too informal?
- Beginning and ending: how badly does it start and finish?
- Structure: are your points in a really silly order?

Use this sentence to get you started if you wish:

> Er … okay! Er, hi everyone and … well, let's be honest, we were pretty hopeless last week, yeah?

Assess your progress

Look at the labels around your really bad speech. Using them to help your thinking, write a list of things you *should* do in a speech.

Reading a speech

You will learn:

- how to use a range of techniques in a longer speech – including sentence variety, repetition and involving the audience.

Activity 1 Examining a longer speech

Different speeches have different purposes. Often they are used to motivate and inspire their listeners. This is a speech given to the audience at Live 8 by Nelson Mandela.

Nelson Mandela was President of South Africa between 1994 and 1999. He had been a prominent anti-apartheid activist, and spent 27 years in prison. He has continued to be involved in human-rights causes, including the Make Poverty History campaign. The Live 8 benefit concerts took place in July 2005, just before the G8 conference in Scotland.

Read this section of Mandela's speech and use the tasks that follow to explore the content (what he says) and the style (how he says it).

'Africa standing tall against poverty':
speech delivered by Mr N R Mandela at Live 8, 2 July 2005

I am pleased to be here today to support Africa Standing Tall Against Poverty, in concert with Live 8.

5 As you know, I formally announced my retirement from public life and should really not be here.

However, as long as poverty, injustice and gross inequality persist in our world, none of us can truly rest.

We shall never forget how millions of people around the
10 world joined us in solidarity to fight the injustice of our oppression while we were incarcerated. Those efforts paid off, and we are able to stand here and join the millions around the world in support of freedom against poverty.

Massive poverty and obscene inequality are such terrible
15 scourges of our times – times in which the world boasts breathtaking advances in science, technology, industry and wealth accumulation.

We live in a world where knowledge and information have made enormous strides, yet millions of children are not
20 in school.

We live in a world where the AIDS pandemic threatens the very fabric of our lives. Yet we spend more money on weapons than on ensuring treatment and support for the millions infected by HIV.

25 It is a world of great promise and hope. It is also a world of despair, disease and hunger.

Overcoming poverty is not a gesture of charity. It is an act of justice. It is the protection of a fundamental human right, the right to dignity and a decent life. While
30 poverty persists, there is no true freedom.

The steps that are needed from the developed nations are clear.

The first is ensuring trade justice. I have said before that trade justice is a truly meaningful way for the developed
31 countries to show commitment to bringing about an end to global poverty.

The second is an end to the debt crisis for the poor countries.

35 The third is to deliver much more aid and make sure it is of the highest quality.

In a few days time the leaders of the G8 nations will meet in Scotland. They will face perhaps the most critical question that our world has had to face – how do we
40 remove the face of poverty from our world.

So much of our common future will depend on the actions and plans of these leaders. They have a historical opportunity to open the door to hope and the possibility of a better future for all. History and
45 the generations to come will judge our leaders by the decisions they make in the coming weeks.

I say to all those leaders: do not look the other way; do not hesitate.

It is easy to make promises but never go to action.
50 We ask our leaders to demonstrate their commitment and not engage with hollow promises. We want action. It is within your power to prevent a **genocide** against humanity. We stand tall as we await your direction.

We thank you for coming here today and we thank the
55 millions of people around the world supporting these efforts. Today should not be the only time we rally in support of eradication of poverty. This should be an ongoing effort. Sometimes it falls upon a generation to be great. You can be that great generation. Let your
60 greatness blossom. Of course the task will not be easy. But not to do this would be a crime against humanity against which I ask all humanity now to rise up.

I thank you.

glossary

genocide murder of lots of people

1 Answer these questions to help you understand the text.

a) Why does Nelson Mandela say he is attending the event, even though he has officially retired?

b) Nelson Mandela shows some of the extreme contrasts in the world – for example, poverty and wealth. What other contrasts does he mention? Write down one.

c) Nelson Mandela describes three steps to ending poverty. What are they?

d) What do you think Nelson Mandela means when he says: 'Sometimes it falls upon a generation to be great. You can be that great generation. Let your greatness blossom'?

Sir Bob Geldof, Live 8 organiser

Madonna with Birhan Woldu, whose plight prompted Geldof to organise Live Aid in 1985

2 To help you with the language in the speech, do the following tasks.

a) You are reading this text on the page. The original audience will have heard it spoken. Give three clues from the text that this is a speech rather than an article or essay.

b) Good speeches generally use a variety of sentences. This helps to create a feeling of interest and rhythm. Find an example of:
- a very short sentence
- a long sentence
- a sentence in which Mandela describes his own experience
- a sentence directly addressing the audience.

c) Find an example of repetition to emphasise a point in this speech.

3 Try these tasks and questions, which will help you to explore the text.

a) What impression do you get of Nelson Mandela's character from the speech? What is he like? Write down two or three points and explain which parts of his speech help you to make this judgement.

b) Explore in more detail the purposes of Nelson Mandela's speech. Some parts entertain, some inform and some persuade. Find an example of each purpose using a table like this. Then write down what you think is the overall purpose of the speech. Explain in your own words what you think Nelson Mandela is trying to achieve.

Entertain	Inform	Persuade
Example from the speech		

c) Which line or phrase in the speech do you like the most? Write it down and explain what you like about it.

d) Which of these two statements best describes the *style* of his speech? When you have decided, explain your choice.
- It is very emotional.
- It is very unemotional.

4 If you were invited to give a speech to students finishing Year 6, what advice would you give them? Think about what the first and last paragraphs of your speech might be, then have a go at writing them. Your first paragraph might be chiefly aimed at entertaining and informing (e.g. about who you are). Your last paragraph might be designed more to give your audience advice to help them in the coming year.

Assess your progress

Look again at the variety of sentences listed in question 2b. Draw arrows to your speech from task 4 showing where you have used these devices.

10

Comparing speeches

You will learn:

- **how to compare two texts on a similar theme**
- **about the language differences in texts of different periods.**

You are about to read two controversial speeches. Both were made on the eve of war. The first is by Major Tim Collins just before allied soldiers invaded Iraq in 2003. The second was written by Shakespeare for his character Henry V as he addresses his soldiers the night before the Battle of Agincourt (1415).

Activity 1 Making a comparison of two speeches

Use the prompts that follow to explore and compare these speeches.

We go to liberate, not to conquer. We will not fly our flags in their country. We are entering Iraq to free a people and the only flag that will be flown in that ancient land is their own. Show respect for them.

5 There are some who are alive at this moment who will not be alive shortly. Those who do not wish to go on that journey, we will not send. As for the others, I expect you to rock their world. Wipe them out if that is what they choose. But if you are ferocious in battle remember to be **magnanimous** in
10 victory.

Iraq is steeped in history. It is the site of the Garden of Eden, of the Great Flood and the birthplace of Abraham. Tread lightly there. You will see things that no man could pay to see and you will have to go a long way to find a more decent, generous
15 and upright people than the Iraqis. You will be embarrassed by their hospitality even though they have nothing. Don't treat them as refugees for they are in their own country. Their children will be poor. In years to come they will know that the light of liberation in their lives was brought by you.

20 If there are casualties of war, then remember that when they woke up and got dressed in the morning they did not plan to die this day. Allow them dignity in death. Bury them properly and mark their graves.

It is my foremost intention to bring every single one of you out
25 alive but there may be people among us who will not see the end of this campaign. We will put them in their sleeping bags and send them back. There will be no time for sorrow.

glossary
magnanimous
generous

Text A

Major Tim Collins

1 Answer these questions to help you understand Text A.

   a) Look at the opening sentence. What is the difference between 'conquer' and 'liberate'?

   b) In the second paragraph, what does Collins mean when he says 'Those who do not wish to go on that journey, we will not send'?

   c) What is another way of saying 'steeped in history' (line 11)?

   d) How does Collins show that Iraq is 'steeped in history'? Give one example.

   e) How does Collins ask his soldiers to treat the Iraqi people? Give three examples.

   f) What does Collins mean when he says 'there may be people among us who will not see the end of this campaign' (line 25)?

2 Answer these questions to help you respond to Text A.

   a) When Collins talks about the risk of casualties, he says: 'We will put them in their sleeping bags and send them back.' How do you respond to the words 'sleeping bags'?

   b) Compare how Collins refers to the possible death of his soldiers in the last paragraph with the possible death of Iraqi people in the second paragraph.

   c) What is the purpose of this speech? To inform, to advise, to persuade or to describe? Write one or two sentences to explain your answer.

3 This speech is controversial. Some people admire it; others hate it. In your own words:

   a) explain why you think it is controversial

   b) say what you like/dislike about it.

King Henry V

This day is called the feast of Crispian:
He that outlives this day, and comes safe home,
Will stand a tip-toe when the day is named,
And rouse him at the name of Crispian.
He that shall live this day, and see old age,   5
Will yearly on the vigil feast his neighbours,
And say 'Tomorrow is Saint Crispian:'
Then will he strip his sleeve and show his scars.
And say 'These wounds I had on Crispin's day.'
Old men forget: yet all shall be forgot,   10
But he'll remember with advantages
What feats he did that day: then shall our names.
Familiar in his mouth as household words
Harry the king, Bedford and Exeter,
Warwick and Talbot, Salisbury and Gloucester,   15
Be in their flowing cups freshly remember'd.
This story shall the good man teach his son;
And Crispin Crispian shall ne'er go by,
From this day to the ending of the world,
But we in it shall be remember'd;   20
We few, we happy few, we band of brothers;
For he today that sheds his blood with me
Shall be my brother; be he ne'er so vile,
This day shall gentle his condition:
And gentlemen in England now a-bed   25
Shall think themselves accursed they were not here,
And hold their manhoods cheap whiles any speaks
That fought with us upon Saint Crispin's day.

Text B

4 Answer these questions to help you respond to Text B.

a) In the first part of the speech, what does King Henry mean by 'He that
   outlives this day, and comes safe home, / Will stand a tip-toe when the
   day is named'?

b) What three things does King Henry say the soldiers will do when they
   become old men each St Crispin's day?

c) Who are 'We few, we happy few, we band of brothers' (line 21)? Why
   does Henry refer to them in this way?

d) Look at the final four lines. What will those men who aren't in the
   battle think on each St Crispin's Day in the future?

e) What clues are there that this text was written a long time ago?

f) What is the purpose of this speech? To inform, to advise, to persuade
   or to describe? Write a sentence or two explaining your answer.

5 To help you compare the texts, list three to five things that you think:
   a) these texts have in common
   b) make them seem very different.

6 For each of the statements in the table below, write in a copy of the table whether it applies to:
   ● Text A   ● both
   ● Text B   ● neither.

For all the statements that apply to both speeches, write down one quotation and a sentence or two that explain their effect on the listener.

Statement	A / B / both / neither
a) The main purpose of the speaker is to persuade his listeners.	
b) The speaker uses lots of repetition.	
c) The speech makes war seem heroic and glorious.	
d) The speech reminds soldiers of their responsibilities.	
e) The speech warns that the battle will not be easy and some people will die.	
f) The speech explains what will happen if the battle is lost.	
g) The speech uses complex language.	

7 Some people say that texts like these should not be used in schools because they appear to glorify war. What is your opinion?

8 Which speech do you prefer and why?

Assess your progress

For each sentence, tick the box that you feel applies to your understanding of Texts A and B.

	Er… no, not really	I think so	I'm sure of it
I understand what Text A is about.			
I understand what Text B is about.			
I can say where, in both texts, the speaker is being persuasive.			
I can comment on how the writer's choice of language makes the speech persuasive.			
I can compare the two texts, explaining the ways in which they are similar and different.			

Rhetorical devices

Rhetorical devices are language techniques that speech writers use to help persuade their audience of the points they are making.

Look at these examples taken from well known speeches. Each demonstrates one of the following rhetorical devices.

- Alliteration: one or more words that begin with the same sound.
- Contrast: opposites, or opposing ideas.
- Repetition: the same word or phrase repeated.
- Rhetorical question: a question the audience is not expected to answer.
- Lists of three: three related words or phrases, one after the other.
- Emotional appeal: a phrase or sentence appealing to the audience's emotions.
- Facts and statistics: evidence to make the speaker's point more believable.

1 Which example below demonstrates which rhetorical device?

  A Abraham Lincoln: 'Government of the people, by the people, for the people.'

  B George W Bush: 'More than half the people of our world live in democratic nations.'

  C Julius Caesar: 'Veni, vidi, vici' ('I came, I saw, I conquered').

  D Martin Luther King: 'I have a dream that my four little children will one day live in a nation where they will not be judged by the colour of their skin.'

  E Shylock (from *The Merchant of Venice* by Shakespeare: 'If you prick us, do we not bleed; if you tickle us, do we not laugh? If you poison us, do we not die?'

  F Tony Blair: 'My three priorities for government would be education, education and education.'

  G Winston Churchill: 'Now this is not the end. It is not even the beginning of the end. But it is, perhaps, the end of the beginning.'

2 Imagine you have been asked to write a speech on one of these subjects:

  * the importance of recycling
  * television should be banned
  * eat five portions of fruit or vegetables every day.

Write up to five sentences that could be included in your speech. In each one, try to demonstrate a different rhetorical device.

Assessment task

1 Read each of the three texts, then answer these questions.

a) Who was worst affected in this outbreak of plague?

b) What percentage of London's population died?

c) What one thing may have brought this outbreak of plague to an end?

A certain lady had an only daughter, a young maiden about nineteen years old, and who was possessed of a very considerable fortune. They were only lodgers in the house where they were. The young woman, her mother, and the maid had been **abroad** on some occasion, but about two hours after they came home the young lady complained she was not well; in a quarter of an hour more she vomited and had a violent pain in her head. 'Pray God,' says her mother, in a terrible fright, 'my child has not the **distemper**!' The pain in her head increasing, her mother ordered the bed to be warmed, and resolved to put her to bed, and prepared to give her things to sweat, which was the ordinary remedy to be taken when the first apprehensions of the distemper began.

While the bed was airing, the mother undressed the young woman and just as she was laid down in the bed, she, looking upon her body with a candle, immediately discovered the fatal tokens on the inside of her thighs. Her mother, not being able to contain herself, threw down her candle and shrieked out in such a frightful manner that it was enough to place horror upon the stoutest heart in the world; nor was it one scream or one cry, but the fright having seized her spirits, she fainted first, then recovered, then ran all over the house, up the stairs and down the stairs, like one distracted, and indeed really was distracted, and continued screeching and crying out for several hours. As to the young maiden, she was a dead corpse from that moment, for the gangrene which occasions the spots had spread over her whole body, and she died in less than two hours.

Text B: adapted from *A Journal of the Plague Year* by Daniel Defoe

Epidemic of plague that ravaged London, killing more than 75,000 of a total population estimated at 460,000. As early as 1625, 40,000 Londoners had died of the plague, but this was the worst and the last of the epidemics. Most of the devastation was in the city's outskirts, in areas where the poor were densely crowded. The disease spread throughout the country, but from 1667 only sporadic cases appeared until 1679. The plague's decline was attributed to various causes, including the Great Fire of London.

Text A: 'Great Plague of London (1664–66)', Britannica online

d) What symptoms of the plague does the young woman have?

e) What cure is usually given when the plague symptoms first show?

f) What does Defoe mean by 'the fatal tokens' that appear on the young woman?

g) How long does it take for the young woman to die from the first appearance of the plague symptoms?

glossary

abroad out of the house

distemper the plague

Assessment task

The Plague

The first case of what was to become the Great Plague of London was discovered in April 1665, in St Giles-in-the-Fields, a built-up area just to the west of the walled City. By the end of May, eleven people had been infected – enough to cause alarm. Victims were shut into their houses, and the doors were nailed shut and marked with a large red cross. Nurses were hired to take in food and carry out basic care, and guards were set on watch to make sure that the sick (or their families) did not escape.

An exodus began. The rich left the city and most of the physicians went with them. Many clergy left too. The king and his court decamped to Salisbury. The poor, on the other hand, were forbidden to leave London. Seen as carriers of the disease, they were turned back at the boundaries.

Attempts at prevention

The people tried desperately to protect themselves. They sniffed herbs and nosegays to drive out the bad air. They fasted and prayed. Apothecaries did a brisk trade in preventative potions and religious and magical amulets. Meanwhile, the Privy Council closed inns and lodging houses. Many markets were cancelled and street stalls banned. Some 40,000 dogs and 80,000 cats were slaughtered. This last move actually made things worse, as the plague-carrying rats were now free of predators. By the end of July, more than 1000 Londoners were dying each week.

Bells tolled continually, announcing new deaths. In September, matters worsened. Thousands died in the first week and carts went round London, collecting the dead bodies and taking them to newly dug plague pits on the capital's edges. Ten thousand people camped on boats anchored in the Thames, hoping to escape the contagion. Fires were lit outside every sixth house and kept burning for days and nights, in the hope that the fumes would drive away the infected air.

Text C: 'The Story of the Plague', Channel 4 History

> h) What was done to prevent the spread of disease? List five things.
>   Did any of these make a difference?
>
> i) What did people do to protect themselves from disease? List three things.
>
> j) Why were guards needed on the streets of London?
>
> k) What was done with all the dead bodies?

2 Using the information you have gathered from Texts A, B and C, write an extract from the autobiography of someone who lived through the Great Plague of London in 1665. You might describe a walk through the city and the sights they see there, or an outbreak of plague in their house or a neighbour's house.

Remember to:
- grab the reader's attention with your opening sentence
- use a variety of sentences – long and short
- use descriptive language to draw a vivid and engaging picture
- find five writing techniques you have learned about in this unit and include them in your writing.

This unit looks at information and instruction texts. It includes:

- leaflets
- holiday brochures
- advice booklets
- recipes
- instructions
- guides.

You will learn:

- how to create an effective leaflet
- how to give clear instructions
- how to communicate information effectively.

3 Information and instructions

Getting started

Think about how you write instructions. Imagine someone has asked you to do one of the following things. Write the first paragraph of your response:

- how to get from this classroom to reception
- how to tie a shoelace
- how to save money.

1

Exploring information leaflets

You will learn:

- how to present information in a leaflet
- about the features of a successful and unsuccessful leaflet.

Leaflets are designed to give people information in an interesting or attractive way. A good leaflet will have a clear sense of purpose (what it's designed to achieve) and audience (who it's aimed at).

Activity 1 Exploring the text type

1 Use a spider diagram to jot down all the leaflets you remember seeing in the past week. They might be in supermarkets, school, a club you belong to or delivered through your letter box.

Where would we be without our teeth? The BDA Dental Museum tells the fascinating story of how people have looked after their teeth - or not! - in the past.

The BDA Dental Museum has the largest collection of dental heritage in the UK. The Museum houses over 30,000 objects and images telling the story of how dentistry has developed from a marketplace spectacle to the complex procedures and treatment of today.

From 19th century dental floss to toothache cures, clockwork drills to toothpaste adverts, there is more to discover than you might imagine.

Dentures

Artificial teeth were popular with the wealthy; they were made from ivory, porcelain and vulcanite (a type of rubber).

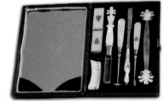

Inside the BDA Dental Museum   *Extraction tools*   *Dentist's equipment case with instrument handles of ivory, ebony and mother of pearl*

Dentistry in the Middle Ages

Until the 19th century anyone could extract a tooth - including blacksmiths, jewellers, wigmakers and surgeons; all without the aid of any anaesthetic!

Come and see dentures made with ivory bases and real teeth reputedly taken from soldiers killed at the Battle of Waterloo.

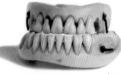

Real teeth were also extracted from the mouths of poor children and 'transplanted' into the gaping mouths of the wealthy.

2 Choose just one leaflet you can remember. Write down what you think its purpose was (what was it trying to do?) and who you think it was aimed at (young people, children, older people, people with specialist knowledge?).

Activity 2   Looking at a leaflet

Look at this leaflet for the British Dental Association (BDA) Museum in London.

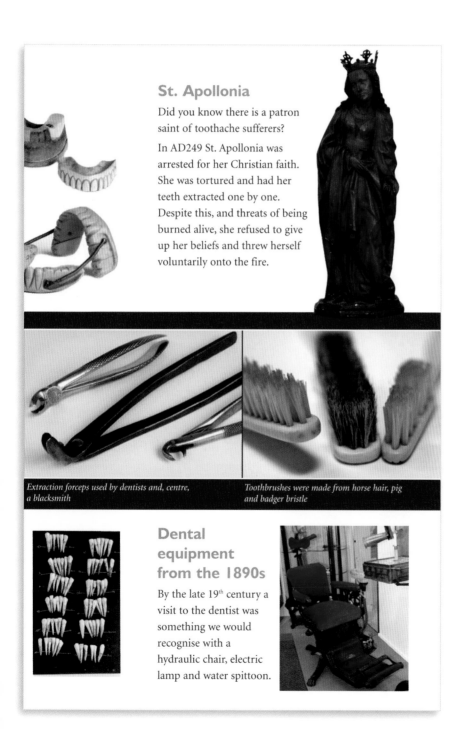

St. Apollonia

Did you know there is a patron saint of toothache sufferers?

In AD249 St. Apollonia was arrested for her Christian faith. She was tortured and had her teeth extracted one by one. Despite this, and threats of being burned alive, she refused to give up her beliefs and threw herself voluntarily onto the fire.

Extraction forceps used by dentists and, centre, a blacksmith

Toothbrushes were made from horse hair, pig and badger bristle

Dental equipment from the 1890s

By the late 19th century a visit to the dentist was something we would recognise with a hydraulic chair, electric lamp and water spittoon.

1 Think what the BDA leaflet is about (its content).

   a) What do we learn about how big the BDA Museum is?

   b) What did artificial teeth used to be made from?

   c) Why is St Apollonia the patron saint of toothache sufferers?

   d) How did she die?

   e) What happened to the teeth of poor children in the nineteenth century?

2 Think how the leaflet is presented (its format). Write down five things you notice about how the leaflet has been designed. You might comment on:

   - the colour scheme
   - the choice of images
   - the number of images
   - the use of headings
   - the amount of text on the page
   - the format of the leaflet (landscape, folded in three).

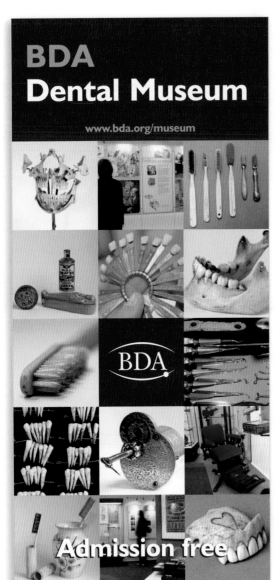

3 Think about who the leaflet is aimed at.

   a) What age group do you think the leaflet is for? How can you tell?

   b) Is the leaflet for people who already know about the topic or for general readers? How can you tell?

   c) What is this leaflet aiming to do? Is the writer aiming to inform, persuade or advise the reader? How can you tell? Write down one piece of evidence for each purpose you identify.

   d) Now you have identified the audience and purpose of this leaflet, how successful do you think it would be in achieving that purpose for its audience? Write two or three sentences explaining how the leaflet's language and design might appeal to this audience.

Activity 3 Reviewing the leaflet

Imagine the BDA has asked you to give it feedback on the leaflet. It is keen to attract more 11–16-year-olds to visit the museum and would like your advice. What would you say? Write an email to the Director of the BDA stating:
- what you like/dislike about the leaflet
- how you think it could be improved.

Activity 4 Redesigning the leaflet

1. Using a blank sheet of A4 paper, redesign the BDA's leaflet to make it more attractive for a younger target audience. Sketch out what it would look like. Think about:
   - the colour scheme
   - the choice of images
   - the use of headings.

2. Draft some sample text. Think about:
   - the amount of text on the page
   - the language you will use to appeal to your target audience.

3. Finally, use bullet points to summarise the main features of your new design. You could use arrows to link these to the leaflet itself.

Activity 5 Marketing your school

Imagine your school is thinking of marketing itself as available for camping in the summer holidays. Without actually designing the leaflet, brainstorm what you think would be good and bad ideas for the content of the leaflet and how it should be designed. Make notes about:
- the audience your leaflet will be aimed at
- what points you might include (for example, things about your school you would mention – the grounds, local sites of interest)
- some good ideas for the design of the leaflet (colour, images, text styles, logos)
- some bad ideas for the design of the leaflet (such as what it should *not* look like).

Assess your progress

What have you learnt about leaflets? What would be your top three dos and don'ts for putting together an information leaflet?

2

Exploring holiday brochures

You will learn:
• how to write a holiday brochure that works.

In the past, holiday brochures were one of the main texts that people used to plan and book a holiday, especially if they were visiting another country. These days, people also have the choice of specialist holiday channels on television and thousands of websites.

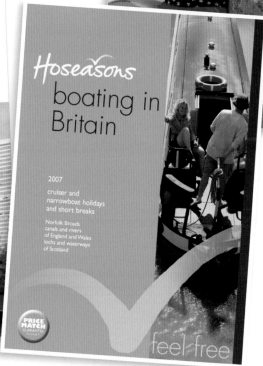

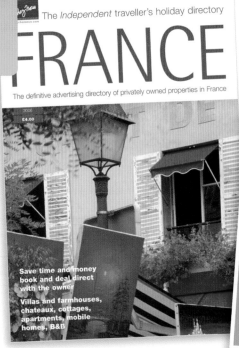

Activity 1 Why brochures?

Think about the differences between a holiday brochure, TV channel and website. Copy and complete the table to get a clearer understanding of the different purpose and audience of each one.

	Holiday brochure	Holiday TV channel (showing short videos of the places it is advertising)	Holiday websites
What is its main purpose – to entertain, inform or persuade?			
What is its unique selling point (the feature that makes it most special)?			
What are its three main differences from the other two media?			
Who might use it?			

Activity 2 Looking at holiday brochures

Look at the extracts from holiday brochures on this page and page 80. Use the questions to explore how they are aimed at different audiences.

THE ADVENTURE STARTS HERE!

Scotland is made for all-season active holidays. Now is the time to follow your heart and try something new – just plug into the resources of Scotland's varied activity providers and develop your enthusiasm. Riding, canoeing, golf – it doesn't really matter, just be sure that Scotland has the terrain and the expertise to deliver a great activities experience, whatever you choose.

FACT FILE

WALKING
Routes, walking holidays, special offers and more:
www.visitscotland.com/walking
Great walks through Scotland's forests:
www.forestry.gov.uk/walking
Take a walk on the wild side up the east coast of Scotland:
www.fifecoastalpath.co.uk
Walking routes in the Outer Hebrides:
www.walkhebrides.com
National Long Distance Walking Routes:
www.greatglenway.com
www.southernuplandway.com
www.speysideway.org
www.west-highland-way.co.uk
www.caterantrail.com

CYCLING
Find out where you can cycle through spectacular scenery:
www.visitscotland.com/cycling
Off road cycling in Scotland's forests:
www.forestry.gov.uk/cycling
National Cycle Network:
www.sustrans.co.uk
Network of cycle routes through Fife:
www.fife-cycleways.co.uk
North Sea Cycle Route:
www.northsea-cycle.com
Cycle across the Outer Hebrides:
www.cyclehebrides.com
Cycle routes through Dumfries and Galloway:
www.7stanes.gov.uk

GOLF
Tee off in the home of golf:
www.visitscotland.com/golf

SAILING AND WATERSPORTS
Set a course for Scotland:
www.sailscotland.co.uk

FISHING
How and where you can get hooked on fishing:
www.visitscotland.com/fish

CYCLE SCOTLAND

Facilities and touring options for cyclists in Scotland just get better and better. The National Cycle Network is a signposted series of traffic-minimised (or traffic-free) routes linking town centres and the countryside. For example, Route 1 is the 501 mile (802km) Aberdeen to John o' Groats route by way of the Moray Firth coast and leading on to Orkney and Shetland. This is also a component part of the world's longest international signposted cycle route – the North Sea Cycle Route, which takes in 6000 km of the coasts of Europe bordering the North Sea, including the east coast of Scotland.

Forestry roads, former railway trackbeds and rural roads all play their part in offering cyclists route choice in Scotland. Mountain bikers enjoy forest parks such as Glentress near Peebles in the Scottish Borders – one of the most popular areas for mountain biking in the whole of Scotland with trails for all levels of experience. To service the growing market, cycle holiday operators offer bespoke holidays, both on and off road. There are also plenty of cycle hire establishments, both in town and country.

1 Look at the brochure extract for Scotland.

a) Write down two activities that the brochure says Scotland is good for.

b) Think of another word that means 'terrain'. Why has the writer chosen this word?

c) What is special about the 501-mile cycle route?

d) What is one of the most popular areas for mountain biking?

e) How does the brochure try to appeal to people with different interests and levels of expertise?

f) Why do you think this particular image has been chosen for the brochure?

Hotel Luxor

✓ ✓ ✓ ✓ PLUS

A little piece of Egypt combines with some Las Vegas magic to offer a truly spectacular hotel with first class facilities.

The Hotel Luxor is the ultimate in glitz and glamour. A unique Egyptian theme, dominates the southern end of the Strip with an eye catching sphinx sitting watch in front of the pyramid. The light that shines from the top of the 30 storey pyramid can be seen ten miles up in space. The Luxor has inclinators rather than elevators in places, which whisk you to your room at an angle of 40 degrees! Among the nine restaurants 'Isis' – in Americas top ten, is the pièce de la résistance. While the hotel's 'RA' nightclub is one of the hottest spots in town. However, if it's a flutter you want, head to the hotel's biggest attraction – the casino, which is as wide as the Nile!

location Set next to Hotel Mandalay Bay, on the southern end of the glitzy Las Vegas Strip and within walking distance of a wide selection of shops, bars and restaurants.

facilities/services • 4 swimming pools with children's sections (some seasonal) • Jacuzzis • Sun terraces & gardens • 9 restaurants featuring seafood, steakhouse, Chinese & Mexican cuisine • Food court – featuring McDonald's • 5 bars • Lounge • Oasis Spa* (offers a wide range of health & beauty treatments, guests must be 18 years to enter) • Giza shopping galleria • 120,000 sq ft casino (gambling age is 21 years and proof of identity is required) • Poker room • Race & Sports book* offers wagering on horse & greyhound racing as well as major sporting events • Nightclub* (Wed-Sat 10pm-4am) • 'Blue Man Group' playing at the showroom* • Themed special effects attractions* • High tech arcade games* • King Tut museum • IMAX 3D theatre* • Dry cleaning service* • 24hr reception with safety deposit boxes (free of charge)

board basis Room only.

accommodation Double rooms with bathroom (bath with shower), air-conditioning, hairdryer, iron & ironing board, Cable TV (Pay TV channels available*), telephone and 24 hour room service*. Rooms are situated in the pyramid or adjoining luxor towers.

size 4407 rooms, 30 floors (max), 3 buildings, 44 lifts
*denotes payable locally

Ringed by mountains, canyons and desert, Las Vegas rises like a mirage from Nevada's southern desert. This, the original 24 hour city, is a glittering wonderland offering some of the biggest names in entertainment, first class casinos and superb themed hotels. Where else could you experience the splendour of Paris, the romance of Venice, the style of New York or even the mystery of Egypt in one place? Plus, with daily trips to the awesome Grand Canyon you will be spoilt for choice. Las Vegas – there really is no city on earth quite like it!

2 Now look at the brochure extract for Las Vegas.

a) Think of another word for 'mirage'. Why has the writer chosen this word?

b) What does the writer mean by 'the original 24-hour city'?

c) How can someone experience Paris, Venice and New York in one city? What do you think the writer means?

d) What is an 'inclinator' (in Hotel Luxor extract)?

3 Compare the texts.

a) What kind of person do you think the Scotland brochure is aimed at? Either write an answer, or draw a quick sketch labelling it to show age, gender, interests, single/family and any other details you think are relevant.

b) Now do the same for the Las Vegas brochure.

4 Think about the audience of both brochures. Imagine you have just booked a cycling holiday in Scotland and you receive your tickets in the post. When you open the envelope, you discover that you have been booked onto the Las Vegas holiday staying at the Hotel Luxor!

Write a letter to the company complaining about the mistake. Aim to do the following:

a) Address the managing director of the holiday company (e.g. Dear Mrs Foley).

b) Make up an address.

c) Say what has happened (do this in your opening paragraph).

d) Explain why this is a problem (next paragraph).

e) Explain what you want the company to do about the problem (final paragraph).

f) Finish your letter with 'Yours sincerely' (because you know the name of the person you are writing to).

Assess your progress

What are the three most important things to remember when writing to appeal to a specific audience?

3

Exploring the language of holiday brochures

You will learn:

• about the language used to persuade us in holiday brochures.

Brochures are trying to persuade us to do something – such as book a holiday or travel somewhere new. To do this they often use vivid, descriptive language.

Activity 1 Looking at 'brochurese'

In his book *The Theory and Practice of Travel*, writer Keith Waterhouse describes 'brochurese' as language that does not always give a true flavour of a place. Look at the examples in the table.

'Brochurese'	Real meaning
Brand-new complex	Unfinished
Buffet-style	Queues
Extensively renovated	Concrete mixer on sun-deck
Few (as in few minutes from …)	Many

1 Using the examples above, translate the following extract from a holiday brochure to show its real meaning.

> *At this exciting resort you can choose to stay in a brand-new complex serving buffet-style meals, or you can stay in extensively renovated self-catering villas. Both are just a few minutes from miles of golden beach.*

2 Here's a list of some other words you can find in holiday brochures. Choose between three and five of them, and come up with your own 'real meanings'.

Friendly atmosphere
Busy
Within walking distance
Quiet location
Sun-drenched
Lively atmosphere
Modern
New
Gentle slope
Ideal for children
Thriving resort
Exciting nightlife
Striking views

Activity 2 Looking at descriptive writing

Holiday brochures use a number of language techniques to make their descriptions visual, vivid and memorable. Here are some examples.

- **Comparatives** (adjectives either ending in -*er* or preceded by *more*: **bigger**, **more exciting**).
- **Superlatives** (adjectives either ending in -*est* or preceded by *most*: **biggest**, **most exciting**).
- **Adjectives** giving more information about nouns (a **unique** + **Egyptian** + theme).
- **Adverbs** giving more information about adjectives (**really** big) and verbs (sloping **steadily**).
- **Similes** that compare one thing with another using the words **like** or **as** (**like** a freshly painted watercolour).

Look at these four extracts from a *Chez Nous* brochure aimed at people who like to stay in privately owned properties in France. Then answer the questions.

Like pictures from a book of fairy tales, the pretty Dordogne villages cling to their hillsides.

1. Why do you think the writer compares it to a book of fairy tales using this simile? What picture does it create in your mind?

2. The writer uses the verb 'cling'. What word might he have used instead? What impression does 'cling' create?

'In this wooded landscape there's a surprise at every turn of the road – a glimpse of broad river, perhaps, or a higgledy piggledy roofscape.

3. The writer uses the unusual phrase 'higgledy piggledy'. What word could have been used instead? What impression does 'higgledy piggledy' create?

4. The writer uses the adjectives 'attractive' and 'fine'. What two other adjectives could have been used?

To the north is the regional capital Perigeux, Roman in origin with medieval and cathedral quarters. Here, the attractive towns of Brantome and Bordeilles span the River Dronne, and Hautefort, with its chateau, offers fine views over the Perigord countryside.

5. The writer chooses the verb 'span'. What other verb could have been used?

6. The writer uses the verb 'twist'. What other verb could have been used?

7. The writer uses the verb 'cluster'. What impression does this create of the villages?

But it's the River Dordogne to the south, which lends its name to this department. Rising in the Massif Central to the east, its waters twist past rocky outcrops where bastide villages cluster for defence.

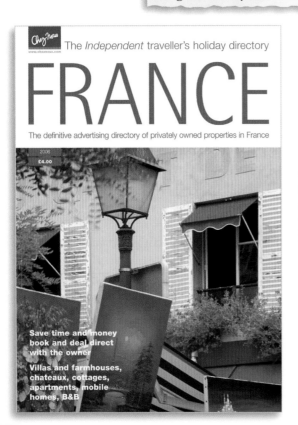

Chez Nous
www.cheznous.com
The *Independent* traveller's holiday directory

FRANCE

The definitive advertising directory of privately owned properties in France

2006
£4.00

Save time and money book and deal direct with the owner

Villas and farmhouses, chateaux, cottages, apartments, mobile homes, B&B

Activity 3 Using descriptive writing

Here's a really bad example of a brochure, written about the village of Stowlangtoft in Suffolk.

Stowlangtoft is a really interesting village. Sitting right on the edge of the A1066 it is easy to drive past it, but if you did you would be missing a treat. The first thing you notice is the old flint church which is proud and impressive. There are fields of cows. There's a really nice restaurant called the Dark Horse, plus nearby a vineyard which has some llamas wandering around its fields.

1 Try to rewrite the brochure to make Stowlangtoft sound a more interesting place for tourists. Use the picture to help you.

a) Change as many words, phrases and sentences as you need to in order to improve the text. Think about:

- details you might want to add (you may have to imagine these)
- the language you use to describe the village and its features – try to include a simile.

b) Once you are happy with your rewritten text, choose three of the main changes you have made. Using arrows and boxes, explain what you did (e.g. 'I decided to change the word […] to […] The effect is […]')

Assess your progress

Write a short paragraph saying what you think are the main ingredients in a good brochure.

4

Exploring instructions

You will learn:
• how to write really clear instructions.

We are surrounded by instructions. Look around the room you are in now and see if you can find examples. They might include:
- learning objectives
- commands
- hints, tips and guides
- signs and symbols.

Some instructions have to be extremely clear because they are relied on in dangerous situations. For example, road signs have to be understood by people who may not be confident readers or may be visiting from abroad.

Activity 1 Giving instructions through symbols

1 How well do you know the Highway Code? See if you can answer the following questions.
  a) What is the difference in shape between orders, warning and information signs?
  b) Describe or sketch the warning signs for:
    - Roundabout ahead
    - Old people crossing
    - Slippery road.
  c) Describe or sketch the order signs for:
    - No entry
    - No overtaking
    - No motor vehicles.

2 Imagine you are being asked to design signs for use inside your school. The idea is to make them as visual as possible with as few words as possible. Think up signs for the following.
  - No eating
  - Shirts must be tucked in
  - Quiet – performance in progress
  - Library
  - Please hold the door open for someone

Activity 2 Sequencing instructions

One essential ingredient in high quality instructions is putting them in the right order.

1 Look at these instructions for transferring music onto an MP3 player. They are in the wrong order and not at all clear. Using the letters against each instruction, decide which order they should be in.

  A Either 'autofill' or drag the songs you want onto the computer.
  B Wait until the MP3 player shows up on the screen (e.g. in the playlist part of iTunes)
  C Make sure the MP3 player is switched off.
  D Once you have all the songs, eject the MP3 player using the eject icon.
  E Plug the MP3 player into the USB port on your computer.
  F Remove the headphones or earpiece from the MP3 player.

2 How good are these instructions? Remember that they need to be clear for someone who has never used an MP3 player before. How would you improve them?

Activity 3 Getting the tone right

Sometimes instructions are personal and polite; sometimes they are much more abrupt and direct.

1 Take a look at the instructions below. They come from a range of different situations. Choose between five and eight; for each one, decide:

a) who might be giving the instruction (e.g. the government, someone you know)

b) who the instruction might be aimed at (e.g. age, male/female, do they already know the person giving the instruction?)

c) what the context might be (e.g. in person, face to face, in a leaflet, on a sign).

Pass the ketchup.	Can I see your ID please?
Keep your receipt in a safe place.	You need to switch the power on, sir.
Return trays after use.	Don't speak to me like that.
No parking.	Oi – stop pushing.
Check your rear-view mirror.	Keep off the grass.
Danger – overhead cables.	Could you wipe your feet, please.
Please leave this room as you would hope to find it.	

2 Now choose five instructions that you can put into a table like this.

Written, very formal	Spoken, very formal	Written, neither very formal nor very informal	Spoken, neither very formal nor very informal	Written, very informal	Spoken, very informal

Activity 4 Writing instructions

Some things can be difficult to explain. Use a mixture of written instructions and diagrams to come up with a really clear fact sheet or leaflet on one of these:
- performing a dance move
- cleaning your teeth properly
- making a really good paper aeroplane.

hints
- Think about the style of your instructions – not too formal, not too chatty.
- Number the instructions if it will help the reader to follow the sequence.
- Label the diagrams if it makes the instructions clearer.

Assess your progress

Write a set of instructions that tell the reader how to write really effective instructions. You can refer to the instructions you wrote in Activity 4 as an example. Think about:
- the order in which the instructions are written
- the language used
- the need to write clearly and be easily understood
- the use of diagrams.

5

Looking at recipes

You will learn:

- how to write really clear instructions in a recipe.

People need to feel that they can trust writers of recipes. The instructions in recipe books need to be clear, precise and definitely in the right order.

Activity 1 Looking at a recipe

Take a look at this recipe for making toast. It is written by Delia Smith, one of the world's most famous and successful cookery writers.

Toast

So I've been thinking, as this is a basic cookery course, why not give the world the definitive recipe for perfect toast? To begin with, I am not a disciple of automatic toasters. The ones I've experienced all seem to be a bit hit and miss, and if you're rather inept at slicing bread (like me), then they're not very helpful at all because if the bread is slightly wonky, a) it probably won't go in the toaster at all, and, b) if it does, one bit ends up not being toasted at all while the other bit is giving off nasty black smoke signals!

1   The key to slicing bread is to use gentle, rapid sawing movements with the knife and not to push down too hard on the loaf. For toast, cut the bread into slices of about ½ inch (1 cm) thickness. The crusts can be on or off, depending on how you like them.
2   Pre-heat the grill for at least 10 minutes before making the toast, turning it to its highest setting.
3   Place the bread on the grill rack and position the tray 2 inches (5 cms) from the heat source.
4   Allow the bread to toast on both sides to your own preferred degree of pale or dark golden brown.

5 While that is happening, keep an eye on it and don't wander far away.
6 When the toast is done, remove it immediately to a toast rack. Why a toast rack? Because they are a brilliant invention. Freshly made toast contains steam, and if you place it in a vertical position, in which the air is allowed to circulate, the steam escapes and the toast becomes crisp and crunchy. Putting it straight on to a plate means the steam is trapped underneath, making it damp and soggy. If you don't possess a toast rack you really ought to invest in a modest one. Failing that, stand your slices of toast up against a jar or something similar for about 1 minute before serving.
7 Always eat toast as soon as possible after that, and never make it ahead of time.
8 Never wrap it in a napkin or cover it (the cardinal sin of the catering trade), because the steam gets trapped and the toast gets soggy.

Always use good bread, because the better the bread, the better the toast. It is also preferable if the bread is a couple of days old.

1 Answer these questions to help you explore the way Delia Smith organises her instructions and the tone she uses to address the reader.
a) How thickly should bread be sliced?
b) How long should the grill be pre-heated for?
c) How far should the grill be from the heat source?
d) Why should toast not be put straight onto a plate?
e) Why should toast not be covered?
f) How old should bread ideally be for making toast?

2 Look again at the advice Delia Smith gives about making toast. Represent this advice as a diagram with labels, showing the key information about width of bread, use of grill and how to serve it. Try to show every piece of information in just two or three diagrams.

3 Think about Delia Smith's style.
a) What does she mean when she says 'I am not a disciple of automatic toasters'?
b) What other word might the writer might have used instead of 'inept'.
c) What other word might she might have used instead of 'wonky'.
d) How would you describe the vocabulary the writer uses? Is it complex or simple? Formal or informal? Why has the writer chosen this style?
e) Look at the length of the sentences the writer uses. Are they all short, all long or a mixture of the two? Why has the writer done this?
f) Look again at the first paragraph. Which of these words do you think best describes the impression we get of the writer? Write a sentence to explain why you made your choice.
- knowledgeable
- expert
- funny
- eccentric
- wacky
- opinionated
- stern

Activity 2 Looking at a different recipe style

Ruth Watson is a cookery writer and hotel proprietor. This is her recipe for coconut pancakes. Compare her approach with Delia Smith's.

I can't tell you how good this dessert is, except I just have. Quite unlike the thin, lacy numbers we eat on Shrove Tuesday, these pancakes are small, wodgy and stuffed with fresh coconut – tropical Scotch pancakes. They have an intriguing slightly chewy texture, and are more than moreish served fresh from the pan with a dribbling dollop of nutty rum-and-maple butter on top.

Coconut pancakes with maple, pecan and rum butter

To serve 4

For the pancakes

100g self-raising flour
half a rounded tsp
   baking powder
55g natural caster sugar
1 large free-range egg
175ml milk
115g fresh coconut,
   peeled and finely grated
1 tbsp dark rum

For the butter

115g natural caster sugar
115g unsalted butter, softened
2 tbsp real maple syrup
2 tbsp dark rum
30g pecans, roughly chopped

To make the pancake batter, put the flour, baking powder and sugar into a food processor and whiz for a few seconds to combine. Add the egg and the milk and whiz until completely smooth, stopping to scrape down the sides once or twice. Finally, tip in the coconut and the rum, whiz for a couple of seconds, then leave the batter to rest for 20 minutes.

To make the butter, put the sugar and butter into a food processor and whiz for about 3 minutes until the mixture is completely soft and smooth. Add the maple syrup, rum and chopped pecans, and pulse once or twice to combine them – don't overprocess. Scrape the butter into a bowl, and keep in the fridge until required.

Lightly butter a large non-stick frying pan, and put it over a medium flame. Spoon in a large tablespoon of batter, spreading it out into a circle about 10cm in diameter. Remember the pancakes expand a little while they are cooking so how many you can make at one time depends on the size of your frying pan – normally, I'd say three.

Cook the pancakes gently for about 3 minutes, then lift up an edge to check the underside is golden brown before turning over and cooking for a further 3 minutes or so. (You might need to ditch the first pancake while you make heat adjustments.)

Serve the pancakes straightaway with a good knob of the rum butter melting on top.

1 Ruth Watson's introduction to the recipe uses some informal words and phrases such as 'wodgy' and 'dollop'. Think about how it would sound if it was written in a more formal style.

a) Rewrite the introduction in three sentences to make it sound more like a traditional recipe.

b) Now write a sentence or two explaining the main changes you have made.

2 The instructions (following the ingredients) use a mixture of formal and informal words. Write down three examples of each.

3 Which of these words best describes the impression you get of the writer from the recipe? Write a sentence to explain why you made your choice.

- friendly
- chatty
- informal
- expert
- knowledgeable
- reassuring
- passionate
- enthusiastic

Activity 3 Writing a recipe

Choose something you know how to make – a favourite sandwich, perfect tea, a pasta dish. Write two versions of the recipe:

a) A straightforward introduction followed by step-by-step instructions that your readers will easily follow.

b) A recipe for the same dish using more of a Ruth Watson approach.

Assess your progress

Use labels and arrows to show three to five main features for each of your texts above. Show how you have changed your language according to the audience – e.g. 'in text B I used "I" because …'

6

Exploring information surveys

You will learn:

- **how to interpret information in a chart or table**

- **how make judgements about products.**

Some magazines and websites are designed to help people judge which product or service is best. The most famous example is *Which?* magazine and website. The Which? organisation runs regular tests on a range of products from cars and digital cameras to sunscreen and breakfast cereals.

Activity 1 Examining a survey

1 Take a look at the findings of the *Which?* 'Survey into breakfast cereals'. What surprises or disturbs you?

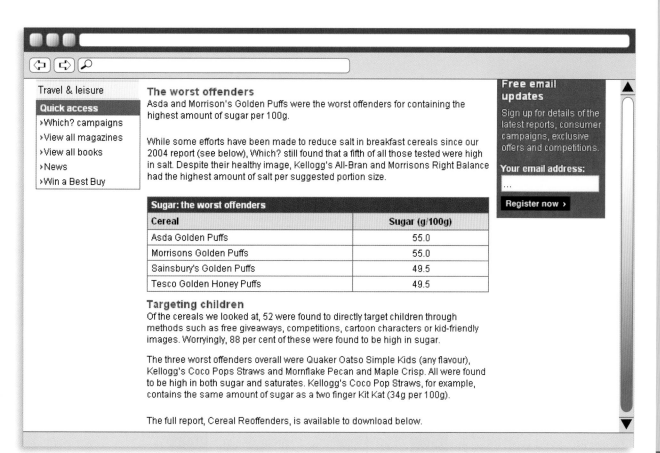

The worst offenders

Asda and Morrison's Golden Puffs were the worst offenders for containing the highest amount of sugar per 100g.

While some efforts have been made to reduce salt in breakfast cereals since our 2004 report (see below), Which? still found that a fifth of all those tested were high in salt. Despite their healthy image, Kellogg's All-Bran and Morrisons Right Balance had the highest amount of salt per suggested portion size.

Sugar: the worst offenders	
Cereal	Sugar (g/100g)
Asda Golden Puffs	55.0
Morrisons Golden Puffs	55.0
Sainsbury's Golden Puffs	49.5
Tesco Golden Honey Puffs	49.5

Targeting children

Of the cereals we looked at, 52 were found to directly target children through methods such as free giveaways, competitions, cartoon characters or kid-friendly images. Worryingly, 88 per cent of these were found to be high in sugar.

The three worst offenders overall were Quaker Oatso Simple Kids (any flavour), Kellogg's Coco Pops Straws and Mornflake Pecan and Maple Crisp. All were found to be high in both sugar and saturates. Kellogg's Coco Pop Straws, for example, contains the same amount of sugar as a two finger Kit Kat (34g per 100g).

The full report, Cereal Reoffenders, is available to download below.

Quick access
> Which? campaigns
> View all magazines
> View all books
> News
> Win a Best Buy

Travel & leisure

Free email updates

Sign up for details of the latest reports, consumer campaigns, exclusive offers and competitions.

Your email address:

Register now ›

a) How many cereals did the *Which?* team test?

b) What percentage of cereals had high levels of sugar?

c) What percentage had high levels of fat?

d) How many cereals were the 'worst offenders'?

e) What do you think are 'kid friendly' images?

f) Why were the results of the 'targeting children' tests worrying?

g) How many 'worst offenders' were there in the 'targeting children' category?

2 How clearly do you think this website gives you information? Give it a rating from 1 (not clear) to 5 (very clear). Then write two sentences saying:

a) what you like about the design

b) how it could be improved.

3 a) Who do you think is the target audience for the writers of this report?

b) Why did the *Which?* team test so many cereals?

c) Why do you think the writers decided to begin by focusing on the 'worst offenders'? What effect did they want to have on the reader?

d) The next heading focuses on cereal manufacturers targeting children. Why have the writers chosen to do this?

e) What is the writer's opinion about cereals which target children? How do you know?

Activity 2 Exploring data

1 The *Which?* Report *Breakfast Breakdown* (July 2006) is a 23-page document giving the full results of its survey. Use one page to explore how to make judgements using data.

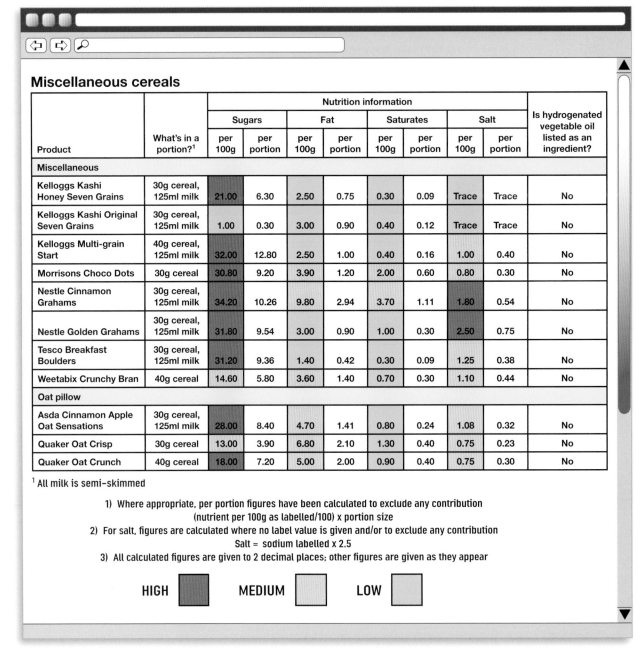

Miscellaneous cereals

Product	What's in a portion?[1]	Nutrition information								Is hydrogenated vegetable oil listed as an ingredient?
		Sugars		Fat		Saturates		Salt		
		per 100g	per portion	per 100g	per portion	per 100g	per portion	per 100g	per portion	
Miscellaneous										
Kelloggs Kashi Honey Seven Grains	30g cereal, 125ml milk	21.00	6.30	2.50	0.75	0.30	0.09	Trace	Trace	No
Kelloggs Kashi Original Seven Grains	30g cereal, 125ml milk	1.00	0.30	3.00	0.90	0.40	0.12	Trace	Trace	No
Kelloggs Multi-grain Start	40g cereal, 125ml milk	32.00	12.80	2.50	1.00	0.40	0.16	1.00	0.40	No
Morrisons Choco Dots	30g cereal	30.80	9.20	3.90	1.20	2.00	0.60	0.80	0.30	No
Nestle Cinnamon Grahams	30g cereal, 125ml milk	34.20	10.26	9.80	2.94	3.70	1.11	1.80	0.54	No
Nestle Golden Grahams	30g cereal, 125ml milk	31.80	9.54	3.00	0.90	1.00	0.30	2.50	0.75	No
Tesco Breakfast Boulders	30g cereal, 125ml milk	31.20	9.36	1.40	0.42	0.30	0.09	1.25	0.38	No
Weetabix Crunchy Bran	40g cereal	14.60	5.80	3.60	1.40	0.70	0.30	1.10	0.44	No
Oat pillow										
Asda Cinnamon Apple Oat Sensations	30g cereal, 125ml milk	28.00	8.40	4.70	1.41	0.80	0.24	1.08	0.32	No
Quaker Oat Crisp	30g cereal	13.00	3.90	6.80	2.10	1.30	0.40	0.75	0.23	No
Quaker Oat Crunch	40g cereal	18.00	7.20	5.00	2.00	0.90	0.40	0.75	0.30	No

[1] All milk is semi-skimmed

1) Where appropriate, per portion figures have been calculated to exclude any contribution
(nutrient per 100g as labelled/100) x portion size
2) For salt, figures are calculated where no label value is given and/or to exclude any contribution
Salt = sodium labelled x 2.5
3) All calculated figures are given to 2 decimal places; other figures are given as they appear

HIGH ☐ MEDIUM ☐ LOW ☐

a) How many cereals are tested on this page of the survey?

b) How many of the cereals are 'miscellaneous' (meaning 'various')?

c) What do the red, amber and green lights mean?

d) Of the miscellaneous cereals, how many have portions of 40g?

e) How many of the cereals in the whole table contain high levels of sugar?

f) How many contain high levels of salt?

g) What cereal has medium fat and low saturates? (Write down one.)

h) Which cereals have both high sugar and high salt?

i) How many cereals are low on sugars, fat, saturates and salt?

j) Which cereal has the highest sugar per portion?

k) Which has the highest fat per portion?

l) Which appears to be the healthiest cereal? Which is the unhealthiest?

2 Do you think this large amount of detailed information is well presented and easy to understand? How else could this information be presented? Write a sentence or two explaining your answer.

Activity 3 Producing a survey

Decide on a product you could test – e.g., types of chocolate (organic Fair Trade versus famous brands), low-fat crisps, MP3 players, types of Cola. Devise how you might approach the tests and how you will present the results.

1 Decide why you are testing these products. Is it to see how healthy they are? Or how good they taste? Or how well they perform their job? Write a sentence or two explaining the purpose of your survey.

2 What qualities would you look for or measure in your product? Write down five or six that you think are most important.

3 How will you get the information you need to compare the products? Will you use information provided by the manufacturer? Or will you need to do some of your own tests?

4 How will you set out your findings? In a table, like the *Which?* report, or a different way?

5 Plan an introduction, like the one from the *Which?* report, in which you give a summary of why you carried out the survey and what you found. Will you just present the information and let readers draw their own conclusions or will you include your own opinion?

You could visit the Which? website to help in your planning.

Assess your progress

Producing a survey like this costs a lot of money. Write a letter to the editor of *Which?*, trying to persuade him or her that readers would be interested in your survey, and that *Which?* should pay for it and publish it. Explain:
- who would be interested in this survey
- why they will be interested in the information you have chosen to survey
- how your method of presenting your findings will be effective
- how your introduction will grab and hold the readers' attention.

As you plan and write your letter, you may find some details in your survey that you want to change to make it even more effective.

7

Exploring reference texts

You will learn:
- how to use different texts to find out information
- how to decide which reference text is most reliable.

Sometimes we use books and websites as sources of information, helping us to learn something we don't know. Dictionaries, encyclopaedias, thesauruses and other reference texts can be very valuable in helping us to find out an essential fact or piece of information. The problem is knowing where to look.

Activity 1 Finding information

1 Imagine you have been asked for the following information. Where would you look? Using a table like the one opposite, be as specific as you can. (Don't just say 'Google'.)

a) The birthdate of Queen Elizabeth I.

b) Facts about the life of Martin Luther King.

c) The meaning of the word 'cynical'.

d) Two words meaning 'nasty'.

e) The title of a famous poem by Emily Dickinson.

f) The name of the 42nd American state.

g) The design of the flag of Turkey.

h) The address of the French Embassy in Berlin.

i) Details of the films playing at your nearest cinema.

j) The cheapest price of a digital radio.

k) The top downloaded song this week.

l) The year Elvis Presley had his first UK number 1.

Fact a–l	Information source	Example (e.g. dictionary)	How reliable is this source of information (* = not very; ***** = very)
	Book		
	Website		
	Other		

2 Which of these pieces of information would be easiest to find out? Which would prove hardest to find out?

Activity 2 Thinking about the reliability of information

1 How do you decide whether a source of information (e.g. book or website) is reliable or not? Look at the table below. For each idea decide whether it is:
- very important (VI)
- not important (NI)
- not relevant (NR).

Book	Website
a) Knowing who wrote it. b) Finding the book in the school library. c) Being published by a well-known publishing company. d) Having a contents and index being frequently used by other students and teachers.	a) Being produced by a company or organisation, rather than an unknown individual. b) Being part of a university (.ac.uk) website. c) Having more text than images. d) Containing lots of facts and statistics.

2 Finish these sentences.
- a) When doing research using a book, the main signs that tell me I can rely on the information are …
- b) When doing research from the Internet, the main signs that tell me I can rely on the information are …

Activity 3 Comparing reference texts

Some people feel more confident using reference books than Internet sites. They believe that because books have been commissioned, written, proof-read and published (an expensive process), they are more reliable sources of information than websites. However, many people enjoy the ease of using the Internet and believe that you can find reliable information if you know where to look.

Look at these two texts – text A from the *Hutchinson Encyclopaedia of Biography*; text B from Wikipedia, the on-line encyclopaedia that everyone can read and edit. Both extracts are about Muhammad Ali, the boxer.

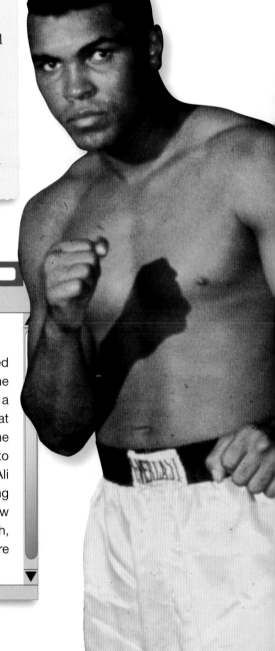

Ali, Muhammad. Adopted name of Cassius Marcellus Clay, Jr (1942–). US boxer. Olympic light-heavyweight champion 1960, he went on to become world professional heavyweight champion 1964, and was the only man to regain the title twice. He was known for his fast footwork and extrovert nature. He had his title stripped from him in 1967 for refusing to be drafted into the US army. He regained his title 1974, lost it Feb 1978, and regained it seven months later. He had the last of his 61 professional fights in 1981 against Trevor Berbick.

Text A

Early boxing career

In 1954, Ali, who was then known as Cassius Clay, parked his bicycle in front of a Louisville department store. When he learned that his bicycle had been stolen, he approached a police officer named Joe Elsby Martin, Sr. and told him that he wanted to 'whoop' the thief. Martin, the coach of the Louisville city boxing program, told Ali that if he intended to 'whoop' someone, he should learn to fight. The next day, Ali appeared at Louisville's Columbia Gym and began boxing lessons with Martin. Ali credits Martin with teaching him how to 'float like a butterfly, sting like a bee'. As an Olympic coach, Martin accompanied Ali to the Rome Olympics in 1960, where he won a Gold Medal in the light heavyweight division.

Text B

1 Look again at Text A. Write down two facts you learn from it.

2 Look at Text B. Write down two facts you learn from it.

3 Text A is factual. Text B tells a story. Choose a sentence from each text that shows its different style.

4 Look at the way the writer of Text A uses minor sentences (sentences without verbs) like this: 'Adopted name of Cassius Marcellus Clay, Jr (1942–)'.

a) How would this information be written in a complete sentence?

b) Why do you think the writer uses this kind of sentence?

5 The Wikipedia entry tells a story rather than simply giving facts. Why do you think it does this?

6 Which of these texts do you think is more formally written? Write down an example from each text to show how one is more formal than the other. What effect does this formality have on the reader?

Activity 4 Writing a reference text

1 Practise writing a reference text. Imagine an entry about yourself written in an encyclopaedia. The aim is to summarise your life so far in about 100 words.

2 Now write a narrative version that tells a story about something that happened in your childhood.

Assess your progress

Use labels and arrows to show between three and five main differences in the two texts you have written. Think about:

- sentence length and type (short or long; major or minor?)
- the vocabulary you choose (formal or informal?)
- the details you include (story or factual?)
- the amount of information you give.

Finally, write a sentence or two about which text is most informative, telling the reader most about you.

Exploring advice texts

You will learn:

- how to write a text that gives readers advice.

Some texts are designed to give information to readers that helps them make decisions in their life. Examples include problem pages, advice columns in magazines and leaflets.

Activity 1 Exploring a bad advice text

Texts giving readers advice need to be informative and reassuring. Readers need to feel they can trust the reader. So it's important that the writer gets the right tone.

1 Read this example of a **bad** advice text. Why is this text not very good?

HOW TO BE SAFE WHEN CYCLING

Cycling is a really enjoyable activity that lots of people like to do, but the problem is that if you don't think about your safety then it can be very unsafe so you need to think about what you wear and how you behave on the road. First, although you may not think it's very fashionable a cycle helmet is an essential part of every cyclist's gear (gear – get it?) because it will help to protect your very valuable grey matter if you fall off your bike. Helmets come in all shapes and sizes (well OK, not ALL shapes and sizes, but there is plenty of variety). There's sure to be one to fit your head. Also don't forget the need to be seen. You need lights and ideally a fluorescent strip or jacket so that you show up at night.

2 Give three suggestions for how you would improve the way it is written. Think about:

- what it says
- the way it is organised
- the style it is written in.

Activity 2 Exploring the language of advice texts

This text is a guide to safe Internet surfing written by the NSPCC (National Society for the Prevention of Cruelty to Children). Using the questions, explore the way it is written.

Surfing safely: tips for young people

Chat rooms and messaging can be great fun. But remember, you never really know who you are talking to on-line. It could be someone trying to trick you, some kind of weirdo or someone really dangerous. Here are some tips to help you keep safe.

- Never use your real name in chat rooms – pick a special on-line nickname.

- Never ever tell anyone personal things about yourself or your family – like your address or telephone number, or the school or clubs you go to. That goes for sending them photos as well. (That way, if you don't want to hear from them again, you only have to log off.) Remember, even if somebody tells you about themselves, never tell them things about you.

- If you arrange to meet up with someone you've only spoken to on-line, remember that they might not be who they said they were, so only meet people in public places and take along an adult. They should do this too, because they don't know who you really are either!

- Never respond to nasty or rude messages, and never send any either! If you feel suspicious or uncomfortable about the way a conversation is going, or if it's getting really personal, save a record of it and stop the conversation. That way you can show someone and ask what they think.

- Be careful with any email attachments or links that people send you. They might contain nasty images or computer 'viruses' that could ruin your PC. So if you don't know who it's from, don't open it.

- Avoid sites that are meant for adults. You might be curious, but sometimes these sites can be difficult to get out of, they can cost more on the phone bill, and they can detect your email address and start sending you stuff you really don't want to get. If you see rude pictures where they shouldn't be, always let an adult know so they can get them removed.

- Agree some rules with your parents or carers about what you can and can't do on the net. It'll save arguments later.

1 Find an example of a sentence that:

a) reassures the reader (helping us to trust the author)

b) gives advice.

2 Advice texts often use imperative sentences. These are sentences that begin with a verb (e.g. '*Agree* some rules …'). They tell or ask you to do something and are sometimes called *commands*. Find another example of a sentence that starts with a verb.

3 Sometimes imperative sentences begin with an adverb, such as 'always' or 'never'. Find an example.

4 How can you tell that this text is aimed at young people rather than adults? Which words show you who the target audience is? Write a sentence or two commenting on the words the writer uses that show the audience is quite young.

5 Notice that this text begins with a few sentences of introduction. What is the writer doing in these sentences?

6 Why do you think the advice that follows the introduction has been organised in a bullet-pointed list?

Activity 3 Write your own advice text

Choose one of the topics below and show your own skill in writing an advice text, using:

- appropriate vocabulary for an audience aged 11–14
- appropriate grammatical structures (e.g. imperative sentences and sentences beginning with adverbs)
- the same structure as the NSPCC text – i.e. write two or three sentences to introduce your advice, then use bullet points to organise your tips.

Topics

Advice on being safe when out late at night

Advice on looking after your bike

Advice on keeping valuables safe on holiday

Activity 4 Finding different solutions

Sometimes magazines ask readers to write in with problems; they then give advice on finding a solution.

My mum nags me all the time. All she ever says to me is 'Tidy your room, be home by nine o'clock, do your homework, blah blah blah ...' We always end up shouting at each other, and I'm sick and tired of it. Please help.

Jamie, age 12

My boyfriend is mean to me all the time. I spent ages wanting to go out with him, but now I'm his girlfriend he treats me like a piece of rubbish. At school he says he'll come round my house and take me out somewhere, but then he either doesn't show up or he makes an excuse, and we end up just hanging around in the park. What should I do?

Lizzie, age 13

1 One of the best ways to give advice is to offer a range of different solutions. That way, people can choose which solution suits them best. Write down three different solutions to one of the problems above. Then, for each one, write a sentence explaining how it will help to solve the problem.

2 When giving advice, you may feel more strongly about some solutions than others. You can use modal verbs to express this. There are ten modal verbs:

- can
- could
- have to
- must
- might
- should
- ought to
- may
- will
- shall

For each piece of advice you offered in task 1, make sure you have included a modal verb that shows how strongly you feel this particular solution should be followed. For example, one solution to Lizzie's problem is to ditch the boyfriend, but how strongly do you advise it? *You **could** ditch your boyfriend* or *You **must** ditch your boyfriend*?

Activity 5 Writing an advice text

Write a final draft of your advice to Jamie or Lizzie (see Activity 4). Remember to:
- include at least two different solutions
- explain how each solution could help
- use modal verbs to show how strongly you feel each piece of advice should be followed.

Assess your progress

Look again at your advice. Use labels and arrows to highlight five important features of writing to advise that you have included. Use the bullet points in Activities 3 and 5 to help you.

9

Looking at explanation texts

You will learn:

• how to explain complicated information in an entertaining way.

Some texts are designed to explain things to us. They aren't exactly instructions because they aren't telling us how to do something. Instead, they take complex ideas and aim to make them simple.

Activity 1 Looking at science writing

Science writing contains complex ideas that can baffle people who are not specialists. Many writers therefore aim to explain scientific ideas in language that most people can understand.

1 Look at this example from the *Hutchinson Dictionary of Science*. It is aimed at general readers.

Space or outer space?

The void that exists beyond Earth's atmosphere. Above 120km/75 mi, very little atmosphere remains, so objects can continue to move quickly without extra energy. The space between the planets is not entirely empty, but filled with the tenuous gas of the solar wind as well as dust specks.

1   2   3   4   5
Hard   **Easy**

a) On a rating scale of 1 (hard) to 5 (easy), how did you find this text?

b) Which do you think is the most difficult or unfamiliar word in the text?

c) How could the text have been made easier to understand?

2 The word 'atmosphere' is used in this text in a technical way.

a) Explain what it means in the text.

b) Use the word 'atmosphere' in a sentence that shows another meaning of the word.

3 Rate the formality of this text, if (1) is very informal and (5) is very formal. What effect is this level of formality intended to have on the reader?

4 How would you explain what outer space is to a six year-old?

Activity 2 Explaining complex ideas more simply

The writer Bill Bryson has written a book called *A Short History of Nearly Everything*. In it he attempts to explain the world around us. Here's what he says about outer space and the possibility of other life.

Space is enormous. The average distance between stars out there is over 30 million million kilometres. Even at speeds approaching those of light, these are fantastically challenging distances for any travelling individual. Of course, it is possible that alien beings travel billions of miles to amuse themselves by planting crop circles in Wiltshire or frightening the daylights out of some poor guy in a pick-up truck on a lonely road in Arizona (they must have teenagers after all), but it does seem unlikely.

Still, statistically the probability that there are other thinking beings out there is good. Nobody knows how many stars there are in the Milky Way – estimates range from 100 billion or so to perhaps 400 billion – and the Milky Way is just one of 140 billion or so other galaxies, many of them even larger than ours.

1 a) Using the rating scale 1 (hard) to 5 (easy), how did you find this text?

   b) Which do you think is the most difficult or unfamiliar word Bill Bryson uses?

   c) What one word or phrase would you normally not expect to find in a scientific text?

   1 2 3 4 5
   Hard   Easy

2 Many explanation texts have an impersonal style – i.e. the author avoids mentioning her- or himself. Find an example of where Bill Bryson writes more personally. What effect does this have?

3 What do you understand by Bryson's comment: 'They must have teenagers, after all'?

4 Although Bryson writes in a personal style in this text, he also uses some facts and figures. Why do you think he does this?

5 Does the extract from *Hutchinson Dictionary of Science*, or Bryson's text, give you a clearer understanding of space?

6 list three features that make writing to explain successful. Think about:
   - the language used
   - the tone of the writing (personal or impersonal)
   - the use of facts and figures.

Activity 3 Writing an explanation text

Take a subject that some adults find difficult, e.g.:
- programming a video to record a programme
- using predictive text on a phone
- downloading songs onto an MP3 player.

Write a short explanation text that explains the process but also aims to entertain them.

Assess your progress

Pick out one sentence from your explanation text that you think explains very successfully. Then pick out one sentence that entertains. Write a sentence for each, explaining why you feel they are effective.

10

Looking at reviews

You will learn:
- how to write an informative and entertaining review.

Some information texts are designed to help us make our minds up. They might be recommending the best book to take on holiday or reviewing the latest film. The aim of reviews is usually to entertain the reader as well as to inform us.

Activity 1 Looking at reviews

1 Look at this compilation of newspaper reviews of the movie *Stormbreaker*, released in 2006.

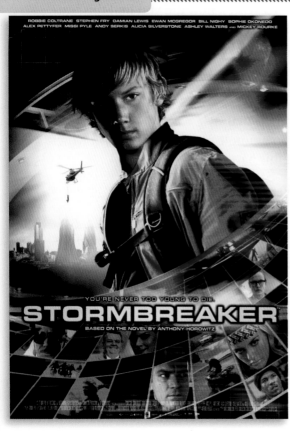

'Daniel Craig must be fuming in his tux,' said Catherine Shoad in the *Sunday Telegraph*. 'Just when everyone was supposed to be getting excited about his upcoming debut as 007, along comes a younger model to steal his thunder.' Teenage spy Alex Rider (Alex Pettyfer) is the creation of best-selling children's author Anthony Horowitz. In *Stormbreaker*, he must do battle with Darrius Sayle (Mickey Rourke), the evil American entrepreneur who ordered the assassination of his uncle (Ewan McGregor). The film is 'such a predictable mash-up of so many other movies, it's hard to know where to start,' said Tim Robey in the *Daily Telegraph*. *Stormbreaker* borrows from *Harry Potter*, James Bond, *Spy Kids*, and even *Agent Cody Banks* without ever developing a style of its own. The stunts are also 'scrappy' and the special effects 'cut-price', said Nicholas Barber in the *Independent on Sunday*, yet the film moves at such a pace that audiences won't have a chance to get bored. And that's surely the point, said Peter Bradshaw in the *Guardian*. 'I watched *Stormbreaker* in a cinema packed with schoolchildren, all of whom seemed to be having a fantastic time.'

Summary from *The Week*.

a) Using a two-column table, write down the positive points these critics make about *Stormbreaker* and then the negative points.

b) Of the negative points, which criticism do you think is the strongest?

c) What does Catherine Shoad mean when she says Daniel Craig must be 'fuming in his tux'?

d) What does she mean when she describes Alex Rider as 'a younger model'?

e) What are we told about the plot of *Stormbreaker*? Would it be helpful for the reader to be told more?

f) Film reviews often refer to other films for comparison. Why do you think they do this?

Activity 2 Thinking about reviewing

1 Here are some ideas for the essential ingredients of a review. For each one, find and write down an example from the *Stormbreaker* review in Activity 1.

a) Using an entertaining or funny style.

b) Knowing the book or film in detail (being an expert).

c) Describing what the book or film is about.

d) Making a judgement about how good the book or film is.

e) Not being afraid to tell the truth.

f) Not worrying about upsetting the author/director.

g) Using unexpected language.

h) Knowing your audience.

i) Not thinking you are more important than the book or film you are reviewing.

j) Comparing it to other books or films.

2 What do you think are the essential ingredients in a good review? Use the ideas listed in task 1 as a starting-point. Add your own ideas to make a list of:

a) the three most essential items

b) three items that you think are *not* important.

Activity 3 Writing a review

Choose a book or film that you know well – whether you like it or not. Write a brief newspaper review that does all of the following:
- entertains your reader
- gives the reader your opinion
- gives specific evidence from the book or film to support your opinion
- gives an idea of the plot – but doesn't give too much away
- uses an interesting, lively style
- doesn't use words like 'good' or boring' to evaluate the book or film.

Assess your progress

Look again at the three essential items you selected in Activity 2 (task 2a). Using arrows and labels, highlight where you have included them in the review you wrote in Activity 3.

Assessment task

A publisher is planning a series of holiday travel books called the *Honest Guide*. You have been asked to write an entry of around 500 words on a holiday destination you know well. It could be somewhere you have been on holiday, or it could be your local area.

These are the publisher's guidelines.

You need to divide your writing into two sections.

Section 1: Informing
Give lots of information about the destination so that the reader can decide whether it offers what they want in a holiday.
- Write a short introduction giving an overview of the destination.
- Give a range of information under headings such as: 'What to take with you', 'Where to stay', 'Where to eat', 'Where to visit' and so on.

Section 2: Reviewing
Write an entertaining review, giving your honest opinion of the destination, so that the reader can decide if they want to book a holiday there.
- Write a short introduction giving your overall opinion.
- Using the same headings as in the information section, give your opinion on what the destination has to offer.
- Write a short conclusion, summarising your opinion and saying who you feel this destination would appeal to.

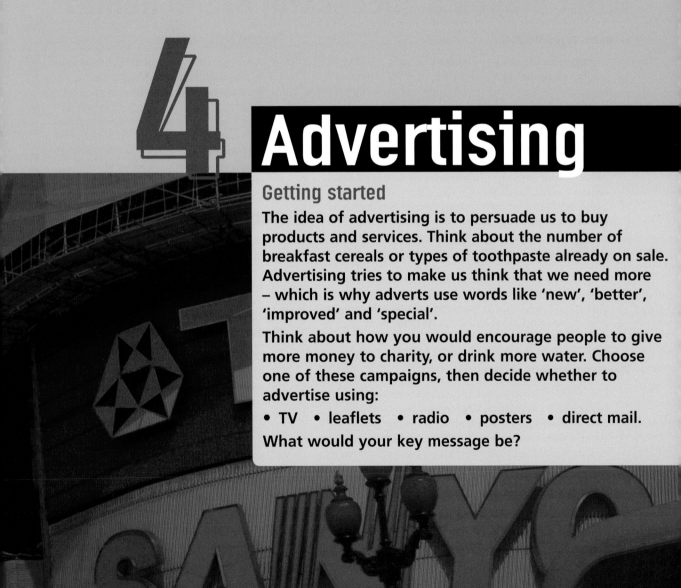

This module looks at different forms of advertising.

You will learn:

- how to write a successful commercial
- about the process of developing advertising ideas
- how to advertise products that aren't glamorous or exciting
- how images and words can be used to persuade an audience.

4 Advertising

Getting started

The idea of advertising is to persuade us to buy products and services. Think about the number of breakfast cereals or types of toothpaste already on sale. Advertising tries to make us think that we need more – which is why adverts use words like 'new', 'better', 'improved' and 'special'.

Think about how you would encourage people to give more money to charity, or drink more water. Choose one of these campaigns, then decide whether to advertise using:

- TV • leaflets • radio • posters • direct mail.

What would your key message be?

1

Investigating brand names

When you think about it, many of the names of products we use are odd. Why are certain sports shoes called Nike or Adidas? Why do people wear t-shirts with the manufacturer's name on, such as FCUK or Tommy Hilfiger? Why are supermarkets called Tesco or ASDA? This section encourages you to explore the origins of some of these names and what they make you think of (the associations they have).

You will learn:
- about the way brand names are chosen.

Activity 1 Learning how brand names are developed

There are many companies that help people to develop product and brand names. Here is a summary of their advice.

What makes a successful brand name?

Clear meaning

A brand name should have an **intrinsic** meaning of lasting significance, **connoting** a class or category of the highest rank.

Creative structure

A brand name should have a creative and imaginative structure. Terminix, for example, is based on the Latin root *termin*, meaning 'to end'. The 'x' of 'Terminix' is based on the Latin prefix *ex-*, meaning 'away' or 'gone'. The new suffix *-nix* further implies negation, prohibition, elimination. The final product, 'Terminix', further exploits the similarity between 'termite' and 'termin' to suggest the complete and absolute elimination of termites.

Appealing sound

A brand name should have a pleasant psychoacoustic effect on the hearer. At YDC we employ onomatopoeia, as in Zip Lock, alliteration (Tinker Toy), rhyming assonance (Nutter Butter) and other rhetorical devices to assure that our brand names stick in the minds of those who hear them.

Recognition value

A successful trade name should be instantly recognisable. Paul Newman's name on his salad dressing line, Newman's Own, is instantly recognisable because of his fame as an actor. Recognisability can also derive from the name of the product line itself, the word for the problem the product resolves and many other sources.

Prestige value

A commercial name should possess the power to command admiration. Products with French or Italian names often command such prestige. 'Clinique' sounds more prestigious than 'Clinic' and 'pasta' is more sophisticated than 'noodles'. The selection of certain words or **morphemes** can contribute prestige value. That is why 'Premier', 'Super', and 'Ultra' frequently appear in commercial names.

Catchy rhythm

Pleasing poetic syllable patterns may add to the memorability of a company or product name. A roller-coaster named 'Super Duper Looper' may sound silly, but people remember the name.

Emotive value

Certain words elicit strong cultural or psychological reactions. Names with 'American', 'mother' or 'family' in them not only evoke positive psychological responses but also can have warm emotional effects on the hearer.

glossary
intrinsic built-in
connoting suggesting
morpheme part of a word

1 Answer these questions to help you understand the text.

   a) Write down one reason the writer says 'Terminix' is a good product name.

   b) The 'Appealing sound' section uses some technical terms. Explain one of these: 'onomatopoeia', 'alliteration' or 'rhyming assonance'.

   c) What do you think 'psychoacoustic' means? Try breaking the word into its prefix and root. Think of other words that begin with the prefix 'psycho'. What do they have in common with 'psychoacoustic'?

2 Interpret the text using these tasks and questions to help you.

   a) Which two guidelines do you think are most and least important?

   b) Think of a brand name that fits one of the guidelines.

Activity 2   Investigating existing brand names

Here are a number of brand names.

Nike	Happy Shopper	ASDA	Galaxy	KitKat	Twix
Fairy Liquid	Mr Muscle	Dolmio	Mars		

1 Using the text from Activity 1 as a guide, write notes about three of these brand names. Remember to include information on:
- the meaning of the name
- the structure of the name
- the sound
- the recognition value
- the prestige value
- whether there is emotive value.

2 For each of your chosen brands, write a sentence describing its target audience. Then explain why you think the brand name would appeal to that target audience.

Activity 3   Developing a brand name

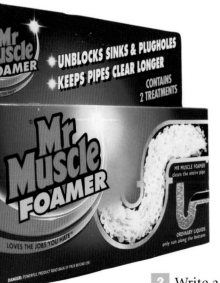

Imagine you have been asked to develop a brand name for one of the products listed below. Remember to use the guidelines from the text in Activity 1 (page 110) as a guide.

- A new phone aimed at older users who want a simple straightforward mobile with no frills.
- A new fizzy soft drink that tastes of pineapple.

1 Think of how you will approach this task. Brainstorm various ideas and choose the one you like best. Think about your target audience. Use a spider diagram to show how your chosen brand name works.

2 Write a memo to the Director of Marketing at the company, explaining:
- the brand name you have developed
- the target audience the brand will appeal to
- why you think the name will be successful.

2

Looking at product packaging: the ideas

You will learn:
- how product packaging creates an image for the product.

Packaging is a form of advertising. With thousands of products on sale in supermarkets, it is often appearance that influences what we buy. The activities that follow explore how different products are marketed.

Activity 1   Understanding product packaging

David Frey is an American expert on product packaging. Read his advice to a soap manufacturer.

> The boss of a soap company in Kenya said to me: 'David, we make soap. It's not fancy. We cut the soap into small bars, which are sold in retail stores. What can I do to differentiate my product from other soaps that are being sold?'
>
> He pulled out some soap to show me. Indeed, it was a simple, no-frills bar. He mentioned that his competitors continually undercut him in price, which he found frustrating. What's more, he didn't know how to set his soap apart from other brands.
>
> My advice to this soap executive was: 'Simply package your soap in a bright fluorescent yellow wrapping with a picture of a sun and rays of sunshine on it, and call it "Sunny Fresh".'
>
> The executive was silent for a few moments. Then it seemed as though a light bulb had gone on inside his head. 'Yes, that's it!' he said.

1 Answer these questions to help you understand the text.

a) The boss of the soap company wanted to 'differentiate' his product from others on the market. What do you think this means? Write a couple of sentences to explain.

b) David Frey describes the executive's product as a 'simple, no-frills bar of soap'. What single word can you think in place of this phrase?

c) What does Frey mean when he says 'a light bulb had gone on inside his head'?

2 Use the questions and tasks below to help you interpret the text.

a) Why do you think David Frey's advice was to make the packaging bright yellow?

b) Why do you think he chose to call it 'Sunny Fresh'?

c) Using a spider diagram, brainstorm some other names the soap could have been called. Try to make associations with the concepts of fresh, clean, cheap, easy-to-use, unfussy.

d) What might you have used instead of a bright fluorescent wrapping? What single image do you think would have more appeal than the sun?

Activity 2 Looking at a product

Look at the packaging of this liquid concentrate for plants.

1 Answer these questions to help you understand the text.

a) What is the name of the product?

b) What three things does Superthrive claim to do to help the gardener?

c) What are we told is in the product Superthrive that makes it work so well?

2 Use the questions below to help you interpret the text.

a) What are the key points that this label wants to make about Superthrive?

b) How would you describe the language used when the label says '50 instant BioUsables normal pure complexes' and 'carbon-hydrogen-oxygen natural organic crystals'? Why do you think the manufacturers have used this kind of language?

c) Write down three things that would persuade you to try Superthrive.

Activity 3 Looking at packaging

Here's what some students thought about the fertilizer packaging above.

1 Write a paragraph outlining what you think about the packaging.

2 Sketch out some ideas for how you might package the product. Keep the same name, but think of what your key ideas would be. Begin by deciding the main points you want to make about this product.

3

Looking at product packaging: marketing toothpaste

You will learn:
- how toothpaste packaging has changed over time.

Toothpaste is a fairly recent invention. It has only been widely used in the last 100 years or so. As a product, it has both of the following:
- **health properties** – protecting your teeth from decay
- **cosmetic qualities** – making your teeth sparkle and your breath fresh, and making you seem more attractive.

Activity 1 Know your product

Here's a brief set of facts about toothpaste. It has been adapted from Wikipedia, the online interactive encyclopaedia.

The earliest known reference to toothpaste is in a fourth-century AD manuscript from Egypt, which prescribes a mixture of powdered salt, pepper, mint leaves and iris flowers. The Romans used toothpaste formulations based on human urine. Urine contains ammonia, which probably accounts for toothpaste being able to whiten teeth.

However, toothpastes or powders did not come into general use until the nineteenth century. In the early 1800s, the toothbrush was usually used only with water, but tooth powders soon gained popularity. Most were home-made, with chalk, pulverized brick and salt being common ingredients. An 1866 home encyclopedia recommended pulverised charcoal and cautioned that many patented tooth powders then commercially marketed did more harm than good.

By 1900, a paste made from hydrogen peroxide and baking soda was recommended. Ready-mixed toothpastes were first marketed in the nineteenth century, but did not surpass the popularity of tooth powder until World War I. In New York City in 1896, Colgate & Company manufactured toothpaste in the first collapsible tube, similar to that recently introduced for artists' paints.

Fluoride started to be added to toothpastes in 1914, but while the early use of fluoride was criticised by the American Dental Association (ADA) in 1937, fluoride toothpastes developed in the 1950s got the ADA's seal of approval. Countries limit and suggest different amounts acceptable for health. Much of Africa has a slightly higher percentage than the US.

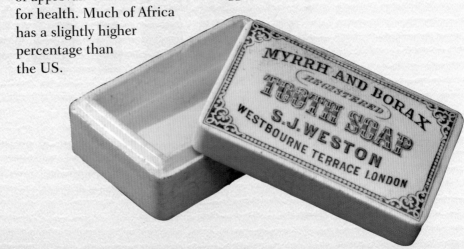

Toothpaste is most commonly sold in flexible tubes, though harder containers are available. The hard containers stand straight up, availing more of the toothpaste and saving shelf space.

Striping of toothpaste is solely for the purpose of an interesting appearance; it provides no functional benefit to the consumer.

1 Answer these questions to help you understand the text.
   a) What did the Romans consider an essential ingredient in cleaning teeth?
   b) Why did it work?
   c) What were common ingredients of tooth powder in the early 1800s?
   d) When did toothpaste become more popular than tooth powder?
   e) What advantage does stripey toothpaste have?

2 Use the tasks and questions below to help you interpret the text.
   a) What did you learn from this text that you didn't know before?
   b) The source of the information is Wikipedia. If you need to check that the facts it gives are correct, how would you do so? For each of the following options decide definitely (D), possibly (P), probably not (PN) or definitely not (DN):
      ● use a Google or Yahoo! search
      ● look on the BBC website
      ● email the toothpaste manufacturers
      ● look for research done in a college or university and then made available on the Internet
      ● use a library reference book
      ● use an Internet encyclopaedia with a well-known reputation.

3 What do you learn from the extract that might help you to make decisions about the following?
   ● How to market the product.
   ● Your target audience and their needs.
   ● How to package the product.

Assess your progress

Think of three different groups of people – or target audiences – who might buy a new brand of toothpaste. You might want to aim at a specific age group or gender. For each target audience, decide on:
● a brand name for the toothpaste
● the key points you would want to emphasise in the toothpaste's packaging.

Show your work to a partner, but do not reveal the target audience for each product. See if they can work out the three target audiences you were aiming at.

Activity 2 Looking at toothpaste packaging

It is important to encourage children from an early age to clean their teeth regularly. These days there are toothpastes directly marketed at children (there didn't used to be). Compare these samples of children's toothpastes.

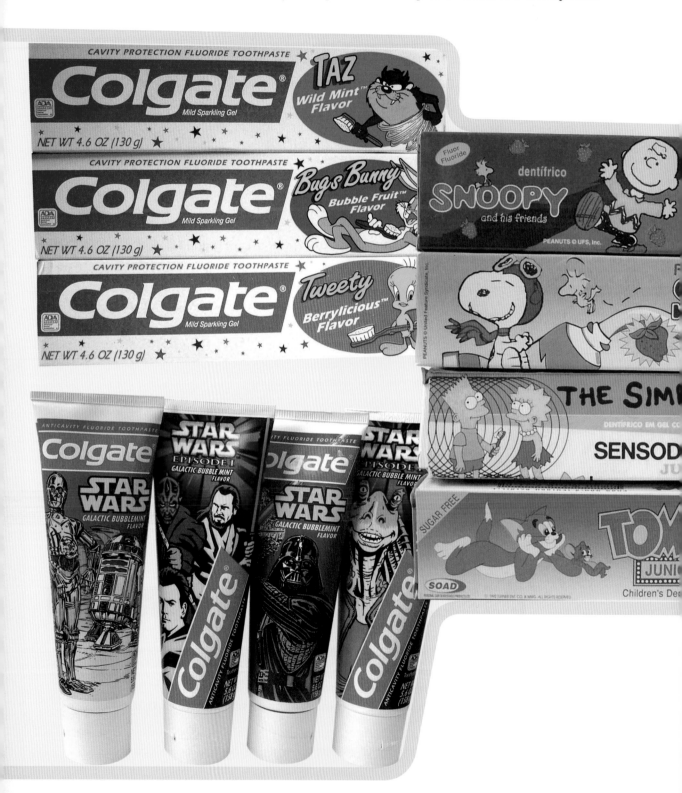

1. Before you begin your comparison, what do you think are the essential ingredients in packaging toothpaste for children? Think of three things.

2. Use these questions to help you compare the packaging.

    a) Which two toothpastes use the brightest colours?

    b) Which do not use images of cartoons/well-known characters?

    c) Which are packaged in a traditional toothpaste box?

    d) Which do not clearly state the name of the toothpaste?

    e) Which do not include an image of a smiling face?

    f) Which include information about what the toothpaste contains?

3. Which packaging do you like best? Give your opinion in one paragraph. Include your views on:
    - use of colour
    - use of images
    - overall design.

Activity 3   Reviewing what you have learnt

Imagine you have been asked by a toothpaste company to give advice on packaging a new toothpaste for children aged seven to eleven. Write an email or letter that tells the company what you think the essential ingredients are.

Use these four subheadings to structure your advice.
- Design of tube/packaging
- Use of colour
- Use of images
- Use of tie-in characters

You might start like this:

```
⊙ ○ ○                                                              ⊂⊃

   Thank you for requesting my advice on packaging toothpaste
   for children …
```

Assess your progress

Re-read your email or letter. Label your writing to show you have covered the four bullet points in Activity 3. Then for each point, label where you have given 'advice' and where you have given an 'explanation' of your advice (e.g. why your suggestions will appeal to the target audience).

If you have missed out any advice or explanations, add them to your writing.

4

Looking at logos

You will learn:
- how logos are designed to shape our attitudes towards a product.

Logos have been around for a long time. The term comes from the 1930s word 'logotype', from the Greek words *logos* meaning 'word' and *type* meaning 'impression'.

Activity 1 Looking at logos

It is often possible to tell what a product is from just its logo, without reading any of the advertising in detail. Look at this selection of logos connected with health.

1 Choose three of the logos above and write down your first impression of each. Try to say something about:
- the use of colours
- the choice of image and what it suggests
- the words
- what you think the logo is designed to make the customer feel.

Activity 2 Learning about logo design

Read through the advice on page 119 about designing logos and use it to answer the questions below.

1 What are the main points to think about when designing a logo, according to Philippa Nettleton?

2 Philippa Nettleton says you need to think about where the logo will appear. What difference would it make to the design if it was going to appear on:

a) an aeroplane

b) paperwork, such as a letterhead

c) both?

3 Think of five different colours and five products whose logos are mainly that colour. For each, write a sentence explaining what you think that colour suggests about the product.

4 The writer advises: 'to come up with one good idea it takes lots of good ideas.' What do you think she means by this?

Logos need a lot of work. Start by getting down any ideas, however random or silly they might seem. First think about the product or company. How should it make you feel – warm, proud, trusting? Does it want us to think it is a classy, sophisticated product or something cheap and cheerful, friendly and reassuring? These emotions will help to decide the shape and colour of the logo.

Think about where the logo will be used – on products, signs, paperwork, aircraft.? Who will see it and how large will it need to be?

Play around with colours. Warm colours like pinks, yellows and reds help to show emotion. Blues might suggest trust and authority, while black and white can suggest clarity and straightforwardness. It's the same with shapes. Curves, circles and ovals can feel emotionally warmer than straight lines and boxes, which can suggest trust, tradition and safety.

Play around with the letters in words. Look at the difference between upper case (authority) and lower case (informality). Try different punctuation – full stops, exclamation marks – or arrows and other shapes.

Be experimental. Once you start combining shapes, lettering and colours, you have a huge combination of ideas and emotions to play with.

Remember: to come up with one good idea it takes lots of good ideas, so keep trying them out. And keep thinking about your audience: what do you want them to think of the product or company? Design with this image in mind.

Philippa Nettleton

5 Both at the start and the end of her advice, Philippa Nettleton emphasises how important it is to think of your audience when designing a logo. Why do you think this is?

Activity 3   Designing a logo

Look at these pieces of product information. Choose one of them and brainstorm some logo ideas, using the advice in Activity 2.
- A new bottled water called PURE
- A new tea bag called REFRESHA
- A new environmental charity called GO GREEN

Assess your progress

Once you have devised a logo you are happy with, write a paragraph explaining your ideas and saying why you think it will appeal to consumers. Remember to comment on each of the bullet points in Activity 1 question 1 opposite.

5

Learning about advertising jingles

You will learn:
- how advertising uses sung jingles to make products memorable.

glossary

jingle simple, repetitious, catchy rhyme set to music

tagline short, final message that sums up the product or brand

Most of us can remember songs and nursery rhymes we learnt as very young children. Chances are you can also sing the jingles that identify well-known brands such as Coca-Cola and McDonald's. Since the 1940s sung jingles have been used to help people remember the name of a product, a service or even a radio station.

Activity 1 Read about a memorable jingle

Read this news article about jingles, then answer the questions that follow.

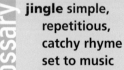

'Just One Cornetto' Most Memorable Ad Jingle

15th May 2006

The Walls 'Just one Cornetto' tune has been voted the most memorable ad jingle of all time.

Now the famous advert - first made 23 years ago and featuring a singing gondolier – is to be remade.

A survey of 1,000 people found that more than seven-in-10 could recognise and remember the ad first made in 1983.

Following the response to the survey, ad agency McCann Erickson has decided to recreate and relaunch the ad to be screened in the run-up to the World Cup this summer.

An ad industry insider said, 'Previously the tune was sung by a gondolier, but this time the ad has been shot in London and features iconic landmarks including Piccadilly Circus, London buses and the marathon.'

The Cornetto advert - sung to the tune of Italian love song 'O Sole Mio' – came top of a survey that featured other well-known jingles such as Shake 'N' Vac's 'Do the Shake and Vac' and R. Whites' 'Secret Lemonade Drinker'.

The Top 10 Advert Jingles
1 Walls Cornetto – 'Just One Cornetto'
2 Shake 'N' Vac – 'Do the Shake and Vac'
3 R. Whites – 'Secret Lemonade Drinker'
4 Kia Ora – 'I'll Be Your Dog'
5 Mars – 'A Mars a Day Helps You Work, Rest and Play'
6 Kwik-Fit – 'Can't Get Quicker Than a Kwik-Fit Fitter'
7 Club Biscuits – 'If You Like a Lot of Chocolate on Your Biscuit Join Our Club.'
8 Coca-Cola – 'I'd Like to Teach the World to Sing'
9 Cadbury's Flake – 'Crumbliest Flakiest Chocolate'
10 Um Bongo – 'They Drink it in the Congo'

1 Answer these questions to help you understand the text.

a) In which year was the first 'Just one Cornetto' advert made?

b) In which year was the advert remade?

c) What tune did the 'Just one Cornetto' jingle use?

d) What changes did the advertising agency make to the advert when they relaunched it?

e) Why do you think the agency decided to make the changes?

2 What do you think made the Cornetto jingle memorable?

Activity 2 Thinking about what makes adverts memorable

Most adverts on radio or television use music and/or jingles. List as many brands or products that you can think of that use memorable jingles or music. Then, focusing on three or four examples, answer the following questions.

1 Briefly describe what the music is and how it is used. For example, what sort of music is used? Does it change? Is it at the same volume? Is it used throughout the advert?

2 Is a jingle used in the advert? If so, what is it?

3 What makes the music or jingles effective?

4 Do you like the music or jingles for these brands or products?

5 Does it matter whether you like the music or jingles?

Activity 3 Looking at taglines

Adverts often include taglines, such as Tesco's 'Every little helps' or Nokia's 'Connecting people'. Discuss some other examples of taglines used in radio or television adverts. Answer these questions about three or four examples.

1 Why do you think these taglines were chosen for these products?

2 Does it make you (or the audience the adverts are aimed at) want to buy the product? Why/why not?

Activity 4 Writing an advert

Think of a healthy food product that could be advertised on the television or radio. First decide what its unique selling point is (what makes it different from other products); and what it might be called. Then think of some ideas for a radio advertisement. (You don't need to come up with a full storyboard.) Decide whether to include the following, and give your reasons:

- music
- jingles
- tagline.

Assess your progress

Write five questions that would test:

- a partner's understanding of jingles and taglines
- their purpose
- the way they are written to achieve that purpose.

Swap your questions with a partner and try to answer what they have written.

6

Exploring radio commercials

You will learn:

• how radio adverts use language to create pictures.

Radio advertising gives writers the freedom to create pictures in people's minds. It can use a range of voices, music and sound effects.

Activity 1 Comparing radio commercials

Here are five radio adverts, selected by advertising experts as some of the best of recent years.

BT Call Stimulation

SFX:	Phone ringing
Hollie:	*Hello*
Max:	*Hello mate, how are you? What have you been up to?*
Hollie:	*We done Mary Mary Quite Contrary.*
Max:	*What's Mary Mary Quite Contrary?*
Hollie:	*(Singing) Mary Mary quite contrary how does your garden grow, with silver bells and cockle shells and pretty maids all in a row row row, and pretty maids all in a row.*
Max:	*I think you've got a good voice.*
Hollie:	*Bla Bla Black sheep have you any wool, yes sir yes sir, three bags full – Mary Mary quite contrary how does your garden grow, with silver bells and cockle shells and pretty maids all in a row row row, and pretty maids all in a row row row and pretty maids all in a row.*
	(Max tries to interrupt and ask Hollie to ring her dad, but she just keeps singing the songs she's learnt)
Hollie:	…(finally slowing) *I'm worn out!*
Max:	*Are you worn out?*
Hollie:	*D'you want me to sing it again?*
MVO:	(BT "Happy Talking" theme music) *BT – It's good to talk.*

KitKat

VO 1:	*…next here on 1 it's Garden Challenge, whilst over on 2 in a moment it's Changing Gardens.*
SFX:	Changing channel
VO 2:	*in half an hour here on 3 it's Ready Steady Garden, but first Can't Garden, Won't Garden*
SFX:	Changing channel
VO 3:	*…ing, but coming up after the break it's a new series of Gardens from Hell*
SFX:	Changing channel
VO 4:	*…and another chance to see Two Fat Gardeners*
SFX:	Changing channel
VO 5:	*and now it's time to join those Vets in the Garden*
MVO:	*Have a break. Have a KitKat.*

COI DTLR Mobiles

V/O: (Both at the same time)	*You're four times more likely to have a road accident when you're on a mobile phone.* *It's hard to concentrate on two things at the same time.*
V/O: (Both at the same time)	*You're four times more likely to have a road accident when you're on a mobile phone.* *It's hard to concentrate on two things at the same time.*
V/O: (Both at the same time)	*You're four times more likely to have a road accident when you're on a mobile phone.* *It's hard to concentrate on two things at the same time.*
V/O: (Single Voice)	*You're four times more likely to have a road accident when you're on a mobile phone.*
V/O: (Single Voice)	*It's hard to concentrate on two things at the same time.*
V/O:	*Think. Switch your mobile off when you drive.*

Toyota Avensis with electronic traffic avoidance

SFX:	Office ambience (throughout)
MVO1:	*What time's the client coming Dave?*
MVO2:	*Two o'clock.*
MVO1:	*That's ok, we've got ages yet.*
MVO2:	*Yeah, have you heard how he speaks?* (putting on a ridiculous high-pitched voice) *Hello Dave and how are you today?*
MVO1:	(giggling, also putting on ridiculous high-pitched voice) *I'm very well Peter and how are you?*
MVO2:	*That's it* (more giggling) *I'm very well and how are you today?*
MVO1:	*I'm very well Peter and how are you? No really how are you…*
SFX:	Door opening.
MVO2:	*Shh, shh.*
MVO1:	(oblivious) *…And how are yooou? And how are you? And how are you? How are you? How…*
SFX:	A long uncomfortable pause.
Client:	(in his own ridiculous high-pitched voice) *Hello David, how are you?*
MVO:	*The Toyota Avensis with electronic traffic avoidance system.* *Be careful. You might get there too early.*

Commission for Racial Equality

VO: *At 3pm June 1995, Everton Baker replies to a classified advertisement in his local paper.*

SFX: Phone ringing

FVO1: *Personnel Speaking, may I help you?*

MVO1: *Hi, good day. I'm Mr Baker calling about the clerical assistant's job that was advertised in the paper.*

FVO1: *I'm very sorry Mr Baker but the job's already been taken.*

MVO1: *It was advertised this morning you know.*

FVO1: *Yes yes, we've had lots of enquiries and we have already filled the post but um, do look out for further advertisements and apply again. Thank you.*

MVO1: *Ok, bye bye.*

VO: One hour later Terry Laing responds to the same advertisement.

FVO1: *Personnel speaking, can I help you?*

MVO2: *Yeah, hi there. I'm ringing about the clerical job that's advertised in the paper.*

FVO1: *Yes, could I have your name please?*

MVO2: *That's Mr Laing.*

FVO1: *Mr Laing...could you...come in at 10.30 next Tuesday?*

MVO2: *Oh, yeah yeah, that would be lovely...thank you.*

FVO1: *Good, you have the address?*

MVO2: *Yes, yes I do.*

FVO1: *Fine, see you then.*

MVO2: *Thank you.*

FVO1: *Thank you.*

MVO2: *Bye.*

VO: *The Commission for Racial Equality fights discrimination like this every day.*
Please report or challenge racism wherever it occurs.

1 Compare the scripts by answering these questions.

a) Which commercial do you think uses sound most creatively?

b) Which is the funniest?

c) Which most directly tells you about the product it is advertising?

d) Which least directly tells you about the product?

e) Which could become irritating if you heard it too often?

2 Write down two or three words or phrases from the commercials that you found particularly persuasive. For each one, say briefly why you chose it.

Activity 2 **Writing your own radio commercial**

Choose one of the topics below, then brainstorm ideas for an original and entertaining radio commercial.

- marketing your school as a good venue for summer holiday clubs
- a new pet-sitting service that you intend to run
- a new coffee with all the taste but half the caffeine

Decide who your target audience will be and the positive points you want to emphasise to them. Draft an initial script, trying to use sound effects and language creatively. Get feedback from a friend, then draft a final version.

Assess your progress

Perform your script to a partner. Ask them to comment on the script using the following prompts, then improve your script using their comments.

- The target audience for this commercial is …
- The positive points of the product emphasised in the commercial are …
- I think the listener was meant to find the commercial (funny/intriguing/persuasive/something else).
- The language used in the commercial helped to achieve this because …
- The sound effects in the commercial helped achieve this because …

7

Writing a press release

You will learn:
- how to write an effective press release

Sometimes people or organisations create news stories by contacting the media in advance to let them know about a future event. Sometimes a news story breaks and a person or organisation needs to give a statement to the media. Both of these usually require writing a press release.

Activity 1 Reading a press release

Journalists receive many press releases. They make a decision about whether to follow up the story or to ignore it. Here's a press release by a junior football club.

1   PRESS RELEASE

2   **28th February 2004**

3   **STOWMARKET JUNIORS**

4   Suffolk football club Stowmarket Juniors have netted their part of a £3 million windfall, thanks to a number of national football partners.

5   The Juniors scored £300,000 as their share of the Community Club Development Programme, a Government funded scheme designed to develop links between the country's leading junior clubs and their local communities. The aim is to provide quality coaching and safe environments for young people to enjoy the national game.

6   Club chairman Susan Nettles said:
'We are thrilled to receive this award. It guarantees our future and helps us to build strong new links in the community.'

7   The award will be formally presented on Saturday 13 March at 11am, before the start of the team's match against Bury Red Arrows.

8   The funding will help the team to develop a new AstroTurf pitch and improve their changing rooms.

9   **Notes to Editors:**
Stowmarket Juniors have been a central part of the mid-Suffolk league since their formation in 1997. Last season they were league champions. Three of their players have in the past 10 years moved on to become professional footballers.

1   Answer the questions below to help you understand the press release.

  a) What have Stowmarket Juniors achieved?

  b) What is the Community Club Development Programme?

  c) Who is Susan Nettles?

2 The text has nine different sections. Match the points below to the numbers alongside the press release.

Heading	Headline	Quotation from club chairman
Topic sentence	Further detail	Background notes for editors
Further detail	Further detail	Date

Activity 2 How to write a press release

Here is an advice sheet for clubs who need to write a press release because they have recently been given funding.

Date:
Always put a date and say whether the news story is embargoed until a particular date. This means that it is not to be published until after that date.

Headline:
Maximum of 10-word statement summarising the news you want to get over in the press release. Do NOT attempt to use puns or jokes you see in newspapers – your job is just to give the information.

Use capital letters, in bold. Centre the headline. Try to keep it to one line.

Sub head:
Use a second headline if there is further information to announce in the press release.

Avoid using capital letters. Use bold. Centre the sub heading.

Paragraph 1 – the introduction:
This should be a short description of the news, written in a straightforward style.

Make it just one paragraph long.

Paragraph 2:
Give a further description of the story. Include as many facts as possible – e.g. the size of investment, who wrote the bid, who will benefit, the reason for investment, purpose, additional social positives.

Aim to use no more than two sentences per paragraph throughout the release.

Paragraph 3:
Give any further explanation of the story.

Paragraph 4:
Quote from someone involved in the story. Place their words in speech marks and say who they are.

Use a quote from a representative from your organisation first, further explaining the story.

Keep to a maximum of two paragraphs for a quote.

Write this clearly, aiming for something a journalist could use directly in a story. Start the paragraph with the person's name and title, so the reader knows who is being quoted.

Paragraph 5:
Occasionally you might want a quote from someone else, e.g. a sponsor, supporter or official. Again, state clearly who they are. More than two quotes in a press release is confusing, so keep to two.

Paragraph 6:
You could include any background about the story (this could also be inserted between Paragraph 3 and Paragraph 4).

At the end of the release:
Always type – ends – (centred).

Imagine your class has raised £1000 for a local charity (you decide which one) by successfully completing a 24-hour sponsored silence. You think this is a good news story for local newspapers and radio stations. Use the advice above to help you write an effective press release.

Assess your progress

Using arrows and labels, show where in your text you have followed the advice above on how to write an effective press release.

Exploring advertorials

You will learn:
- what an advertorial is
- to distinguish between fact and opinion.

Advertorials are adverts which look like newspaper and magazine articles. The activities below will help you to spot their key features.

Activity 1   Reading an advertorial

Look at the 'Choose Cheese!' advertorial from the British Cheese Board.

choose cheese

to look good and feel good!

Looking and feeling good, now and in the future, is a reflection of your lifestyle and that includes what you put into your body. But for a real health and beauty treat you need to look no further than your fridge – for a slice of cheese.

Having a good intake of all nutrients, particularly of calcium, is important in teenage years. Getting the right intake of calcium during these years means we build strong bones and teeth. A lack of calcium at this critical age can increase the risk of osteoporosis (brittle bone disease) in later life.

Dairy products such as cheese, which are rich in calcium, vitamin A and protein, play an important role in any teenager's diet. What's more, cheese is tasty, good for your teeth, skin, eyes and bones and can even aid a good night's sleep.

The recommended daily intake of calcium for girls aged 11–18 years is 800mg a day and for boys aged 11–18 years it is 1000 mg a day. You do not have to change your diet; a 30 g piece of Cheddar cheese (the size of a small matchbox) provides 222 mg of calcium, which gets you well on the way to the recommended daily intake. By adding low-fat milk and a pot of low-fat fruit yoghurt to your piece of cheese, you will easily reach your daily recommended intake.

Strong bones

Cheese has one of the most easily absorbed and concentrated sources of calcium, which is vital to the maintenance of healthy teeth and bones. Cheese is also an excellent source of protein, essential for building and maintaining all of the body's structures such as muscles, bones and teeth.

A healthy, happy smile

The high calcium and phosphorous content of cheese helps replace some of the minerals in tooth enamel – the protective coating on teeth – and further strengthens them.

The British Dental Association recommends eating cheese after sugary snacks and meals because cheese helps prevent the bacteria on the tooth's surface turning sugar into acids that then attack and damage the enamel. And everyone knows the attraction of a bright, white smile.

Bright eyes and healthy skin

Cheese is a good source of vitamin A, which is crucial for healthy skin, eyes and to boost the body's immune system.

A good night's sleep

Despite popular myths that cheese gives you nightmares, one of the essential amino acids contained in cheese – tryptophan – has been shown to reduce stress and induce sleep. So cheese can actually help you have a good night's sleep, essential for looking and feeling great.

Those who think that cheese is fattening will be surprised to know that there is the same amount of fat in a 30g piece of cheese as in a regular packet of crisps. Cheese plays a vital role in a healthy balanced diet.

For those teenagers who want to get more cheese in their diets, the British Cheese Board has come up with some fun and innovative recipe ideas that can be found on their website.

1 Use the questions that follow to explore why this text is an advertorial rather than an advertisement or article.

a) According to the text, what is osteoporosis?

b) According to the author, what two ingredients in cheese are important for teenagers?

c) What does the author suggest teenagers could eat to make sure they get their recommended daily intake of calcium?

d) In which two ways does the text claim cheese can help you to have healthy teeth?

e) How much fat is there in 30 g of cheese?

2 Use these tasks and questions to help you interpret the text.

a) What three main points about cheese do the advertisers want to get across?

b) How do the subheadings in the article help?

c) Write down one fact that you read in the text.

d) Write down one opinion from the text.

e) Write down two sentences which you think are trying to persuade you. Underline the most persuasive word in each sentence.

3 Look at the logo for 'Choose Cheese!'. What image do you think the smiling face, shiny teeth, yellow lettering and exclamation mark are trying to create?

Activity 2 Comparing advertorials and newspaper articles

Even though advertorials tend to look like genuine news stories and articles, there are some things that make them different.

1 Re-read the text in Activity 1, then complete these sentences.

a) I can tell this is not a straightforward newspaper article from the layout because …

b) I can tell this is not a straightforward newspaper article from the writing because …

c) I can tell this is not a straightforward advert because …

2 Answer these questions to help you understand the differences between articles and advertorials.

a) What did you learn about cheese from the text?

b) Would the advertorial encourage you to buy and eat more cheese? Explain why or why not.

c) How do you think the text might be different if it was presented as a straightforward advertisement?

d) What do you think are the advantages of promoting a product through an advertorial rather than a recognised advertisement format?

Activity 3 Reflecting on advertorials

Look at these two comments about advertorials. Which parts of the two opinions do you agree with? Write a short paragraph explaining why.

I like advertorials. They tend to have more text and be more informative than advertisements. You actually learn something from them.

Stephen

I don't like advertorials at all. I can't see the point of them. They're too long, so I don't read them, and I think they're a bit dishonest because they are basically adverts disguised as magazine articles.

Reena

Activity 4 Writing an advertorial

Imagine you have been asked to write an advertorial about a new product. Remember, an advertorial looks like a newspaper or magazine article. Choose one of these products.

- A healthy fruit-based breakfast drink called Sunrise
- A local radio station for 16–24-year-olds called Faze-fm

Before you start to write, think about:

- the key points you will make to promote your product
- what your advertorial will look like
- the text it will contain to make it feel informative and interesting.

You should include:

- a headline
- subheadings
- a logo – perhaps including a slogan (like 'Choose Cheese!' from Activity 1, page 126)
- an image.

Assess your progress

What are the three most persuasive features of your advertorial? Choose:

- one visual feature – the image or the logo you have used
- one structural feature – how you have organised your text
- one language feature – a word or a sentence that will really influence your target audience.

For each one, write a sentence or two explaining your choice.

9

Changing attitudes

You will learn:
- **how marketing tries to change people's views and attitudes.**

Some adverts are designed to change the way we look at the world, rather than sell us products and services. They may advertise charities or campaigns.

Activity 1 Thinking about changing attitudes

Advertising plays an important part in changing people's opinions and attitudes. Think about how you might get people to use less water, or recycle more of their household waste.

Choose one of these methods of communication, than write a paragraph outlining some of your initial ideas.
- letter
- poster
- leaflet
- commercial (TV/radio)
- advertorial

Hands off!

Platform

Children living on the Baku pipeline route

Shell

Thom Scott

Shell's refineries and depots can have devastating effects on the people who live near them. People in Durban in South Africa, Manila in the Philippines and Texas in the US are breathing polluted air, suffering from skin disease and worrying about oil spills. We helped people from affected communities to attend Shell's annual general meeting and put their questions directly to the company's directors.

With your help we can continue to support communities affected by the likes of Shell and lobby for changes in UK law so that they can hold these companies accountable for their impacts on the environment.

Hope Esquillo Tura from the Philippines says "We have brought our issue to the attention of Shell's shareholders and directors and the UK media, public and politicians. For the first time in years I now have hope, and that wouldn't have been possible without Friends of the Earth."

ASDA Wal-Mart

Asda Wal-Mart uses market power to force farmers to sell their produce to them at cripplingly low prices. Both UK farmers and those abroad are affected by this policy. The Prime Minister of St Vincent and the Grenadines in the Caribbean has warned that Wal-Mart's take over of Asda has already had detrimental affects on the islands' economy.

Your gift of £3 a month can make an amazing difference in helping us lobby governments to bring in laws that ensure big companies don't put profits before the planet and people.

Help us fight for a better future.
Craig Bennett

The hands on way to create

"Who really makes the big decisions about our future?

Too often, it's the fat cats and faceless business executives. In the search for ever bigger profits, many companies just don't think about the terrible side effects of what they're doing.

Support Friends of the Earth and we'll work hard getting governments to pass laws to make sure the likes of Shell, Asda Wal-Mart and the Royal Bank of Scotland get their filthy hands off our future.

We're not anti-business and we're only too happy to give praise where it's due. But Friends of the Earth believe passionately that a healthy, unpolluted world is too precious to squander for quick profits.

If you agree, please support us today with a regular gift of just £3 a month. We really are only as powerful as the people who support us. And that's why you can make a real difference by filling in the attached form. Thank you."

Craig Bennett, Corporates campaigner.

For more information, or to join, call us on 0808 800 1111 or visit

Activity 2   Reading a campaign leaflet

Friends of the Earth is a campaigning group that focuses on environmental issues. Look at the leaflet below, which was delivered to households across Britain.

1 Complete questions a–e to help you understand the text.

a) List the concerns that Friends of the Earth has about Shell, ASDA Wal-Mart and The Royal Bank of Scotland.

b) How can Friends of the Earth improve these situations?

c) Who do you think Craig Bennett is?

d) List the things that Bennett says Friends of the Earth believes.

e) Jot down what you think is the purpose of the leaflet.

2 Use these questions to help you interpret the text.

a) What do you think the image on the cover is supposed to represent?

b) Look at the logo for Friends of the Earth. Describe it in your own words. What do you like/dislike about it?

c) Look at the text inside the leaflet. What do you think is the difference between the text in black and the text in green?

d) The leaflet uses lots of persuasive language. For each of the three companies featured, write down:
- one negative word or phrase that describes what it does
- one positive word or phrase that describes what Friends of the Earth can do to help put right the problems each of these companies causes.

3 If you were asked to improve the impact of the leaflet on young readers, what ideas would you suggest? Think about:
- the use of images
- the text.

The Royal Bank of Scotland

The Royal Bank of Scotland is using its customers' money to finance the Baku T'blisi Cehyan (BTC) pipeline to extract oil from the Caspian sea and transport it to the West.

This pipeline, as well as furthering climate change, has been called an environmental and human rights disaster in the making. We've shown that the pipeline breaches many environmental and human rights standards, including standards that RBS claims it adheres to. Join us and be a part of our ongoing work to get the law changed to stop companies like RBS saying one thing and doing another and to force them to consider environmental impacts and not just profits.

By supporting Friends of the Earth with a regular gift of just £3 a month you'll help us publish ground breaking research and expose companies' bad behaviour.

a better future

The Direct Debit Guarantee   ● DIRECT Debit

This guarantee should be detached and retained by the Payer

This Guarantee is offered by all Banks and Building Societies that take part in the Direct Debit Scheme. The efficiency and security of the Scheme is monitored and protected by your own Bank or Building Society.

If the amounts to be paid or the payment dates change, Friends of the Earth will notify you ten working days in advance of your account being debited or as otherwise agreed.

If an error is made by Friends of the Earth or your Bank or Building Society, you are guaranteed a full and immediate refund from your branch of the amount paid.

You can cancel a Direct Debit at any time by writing to your Bank or Building Society. Please send a copy of your letter to us.

our website at www.foe.co.uk

Get your filthy hands off my future

Friends of the Earth

Assess your progress

Write a list of ten things that a successful leaflet should feature and explain why you chose these things.

10

Looking at television commercials

You will learn:
• how television commercials are written and made.

Most of us see thousands of television commercials a year. A survey in 2000 found that:

● 81% of three- to six-year-olds remember having seen the Coca-Cola logo and 69% remember the McDonald's yellow M

● by the age of five or six, most children are aware of the rudiments of advertising

● by the age of eight, children are aware of the promotional and persuasive role of advertising.

Even if we claim not to like TV advertising, it can be hard to ignore it. As well as the 30- and 60-second commercials during the programme breaks, there are also the 'teaser' ads built into the start and end of breaks – often no more than 5 seconds with a quirky, attention-grabbing style.

These activities examine a sample script from Australia and encourage you to think about the impact of advertising on different viewers.

Activity 1 Reading a script for a TV commercial

In Australia, as in many other countries, there are concerns about people putting on weight, not eating healthily and not getting enough exercise. Here is the script from an Australian TV commercial. This advertisement is part of a campaign called 'Get Moving'.

Open on a couple of kids sitting in front of the TV. One of them is slumped in a chair; the other lounges across the armrest. Suddenly, the chair comes to life and forcibly ejects them onto their feet. They're shocked, but soon recover. Cut to see them frolicking with the chair in a pool.

Cut to a girl sitting in front of a video game. Again, the chair animates, wrapping itself around her, and running out the door. Cut to see her playing basketball one-on-one with the chair in the driveway. She's got the ball and the chair is playing defence. Then she jumps up onto the chair and uses the extra height to make a basket. She celebrates with a little victory dance.

Cut to another kid sitting in front of a computer, glued to the screen. Suddenly his chair comes to life, spins him around and zooms him down the hall, then tips him out the door, onto his feet. Cut to see him playing handball against a wall with the chair. We see the words 'GET MOVING FOR AN HOUR OR MORE A DAY' chalked on the pavement.

Cut to our chair character speaking to camera.

Cut to Government coat of arms.

SUPER: www.healthyactive.gov.au

Cut to three girls dancing around with the chair.

Cut to another kid in a living room. He picks up the remote and goes to sit down, but the chair suddenly scoots back, out of the way.

Cut to black screen.

SUPER: Authorised by the Australian Government, Canberra.
SUPER: Spoken by G. Cunningham and D. Williams

Audio
MUSIC: 'You gotta move'
Got to get up to get moving!
You've got to move …
You want to move …
You love to move …
Move!

You ought to move …
You want to move …
You got to move …
Move!

You got to move …
You want to move …
You love to move …
Move!

You ought to move …
You want to move …
You got to get moving!

CHAIR: Check out healthyactive.gov.au and get moving for an hour or more a day!

You've got to move …
You want to move …
You love to move …
Move!

MVO: Authorised by the Australian Government Canberra.

1 Answer these questions to help you understand the script.

   a) What three activities are shown at the start as unhealthy?

   b) What three activities are shown as healthy?

   c) What is the key message of the advertisement?

2 Use these tasks and questions to help you interpret the text.

   a) Why do you think the advert repeats its key message in three different ways?

   b) Which ONE statement about the advertisement do you MOST agree with? Write a sentence explaining your choice.
   - The commercial shows that exercise is enjoyable as well as good for you.
   - The commercial is quite corny.
   - The commercial successfully makes the audience know that they should do more exercise.
   - The talking chair makes the commercial seem as if it would appeal to a young audience.

   c) Use a table like this to say what you like and dislike about the commercial.

What I like	What I dislike

3 Imagine you are the director who received this script. What ideas would you have for:
   - how the children in the advertisement should look
   - what the settings for the different locations should be
   - how the music track should sound.

   Set out your ideas as bullet points under these sub-headings:
   - Children   - Settings   - Music

Activity 2 Looking at advertising guidelines

Television advertising in Britain is governed by a body called the Committee of Advertising Practice. It has strict rules regarding young viewers. This means that adverts should not:
- make children desire things they cannot afford or would not be able to use
- encourage children to pester their parents for advertised products or services (pester power)
- show children in unsafe or dangerous situations that other children might copy
- make children feel inferior, especially if they don't buy the products or services shown in the ads

- show children in a sexual way – e.g. wearing make-up and glamorous clothes
- market soft drinks and high fat/sugar foods directly at children.

Look at these moral dilemmas. Choose one of them and explain your opinion as clearly as possible.

A Should television adverts for toys be banned during children's TV shows, to cut down on the 'pester power' effect?

B Should adverts for junk food be banned on television until after the watershed of 9pm?

C Isn't it the responsibility of parents to control what their children watch rather than trying to control it through banning things?

D Should parents be encouraged to make sure that no one under 16 has a television in their bedroom?

E Should adverts that might encourage rude or aggressive behaviour be banned, even though most people know that they are just for fun?

Using just one paragraph, write your response to your chosen dilemma. Begin your paragraph with:

My view is that ...

Activity 3   Writing a commercial

When a company wants an advertising agency to write an advert, it gives the agency a 'brief'. This brief (list of ideas and instructions) covers every part of the finished advert – from the visuals, to the words and perhaps even music.

1 Imagine you have been given an advertising brief to write and produce a TV commercial. Choose one of these topics, then brainstorm some ideas.
- Persuade students to eat healthy school dinners.
- Encourage young people not to smoke.

Remember to:
- appeal to your target audience
- think how you will make it visual and memorable in just 30 seconds
- test out lots of ideas – e.g. will your advert tell a story, have real-life characters, use celebrities, cartoons, music, a slogan?

2 Now write a draft of your advertisement.

Assess your progress

Write a list of all the features you have included in your advertisement that will persuade its target audience. For each feature, consider how successful it would be in persuading your target audience. Decide whether it would be:
- very successful
- quite successful
- not very good, but it was all I could think of.

If there are any features of your advert that you did not assess as 'very successful', choose at least two and try to improve them.

Assessment task

1 These adverts were used to promote products during the first half of the twentieth century. Neither of them is manufactured any more. Choose one and explore it using the following questions.

   a) Who do you think was the target audience for this product?

   b) What key features of the product does the advert aim to emphasise?

   c) How does the writer's use of language persuade the target audience? Give at least three examples.

   d) How does the image or images used help sell the product?

2 Choose one of these products and design an advertisement to relaunch it. Before you begin, look back at the work you have done in this unit.

   • Decide where you will advertise the product: on television, on the radio, or using a newspaper or magazine advertorial.

   • Make a list of all the features of this type of advertising and the decisions you will need to make.

   • Plan how you will use each of these features to persuade your target audience to buy the product.

When you have completed your advert, write an evaluation of it in which you explain all of the choices you made and the effect you wanted them to have.

This unit explores how television and radio are produced, and the influence they have on us.

You will learn:

- about the impact of television on our lives
- about television genres such as situation comedies and drama
- about the way radio stations target different audiences
- about radio drama.

5 Television and radio

Getting started

Examine your opinions about television by completing these statements.

A My 'must-watch' television programme is …
B TV is better than the Internet for …
C The Internet is better than TV for …
D In an average week I watch __ hours of TV.
E The channel I watch most is …
F The programme my parents watch that I really hate is …
G The programme that I watch that my parents really hate is …
H The first programme I ever remember watching regularly is …

1

Looking at attitudes to television

You will learn:

• why television is so controversial

• how a newspaper article about television is structured.

Some people have very strong opinions about television. They think it can be a harmful medium, especially if children watch it too much or without supervision.

Activity 1 Exploring attitudes to television

The table below contains several statements about television. Read through them, then try the tasks that follow.

A Putting a television set in the bedroom of someone under sixteen is wrong.	**B** Bad behaviour in television soap operas creates bad behaviour in viewers.	**C** Some television programmes are too violent.
D Young people (25 and under) watch more TV than older people.	**E** Television is a good way of relaxing but not a good way of learning.	**F** Junk food should not be advertised during programmes aimed at children.
G The BBC would be better if it had advertisements.	**H** The more channels there are, the more interesting television becomes.	**I** News programmes should include more good news stories.

1 For each statement, write down whether you:
   • strongly agree (SA)
   • agree (A)
   • disagree (D)
   • strongly disagree (SD)
   • have no opinion (HNO).

2 Select the three statements you find most interesting. Give your reasons, using a sentence structure like this.

Sentence opener	A–I	Connective	Give your reason	Give an example	Explain how your example proves your opinion
I agree/disagree with statement		because			

3 Choose one of the statements that you know your parent, carer or grandparents would agree with – but that you don't agree with. Write it down, then explain why your opinion is different from theirs.

Activity 2 Exploring television viewing by children

There are often complaints about the effect television can have on very young viewers. Adults worry that it might teach them bad habits, stunt their imagination and stop them from being good at socialising with other people. Read this article from the *Daily Mail* and see what you think.

The toddlers hooked on telly

More than a third of children under the age of four have televisions in their bedrooms, says a new study.

The figure has risen dramatically from one in five two years ago. One in seven of the toddlers also has a video recorder.

The survey, by the Independent Television Commission, revealed that 52 per cent of under-sixteens have TV sets in their rooms.

The number of under-fours with a TV in their room increased from 21 per cent in 1999 to 36 per cent last year.

Children's welfare campaigners last night said the survey raised serious concerns about the viewing habits of youngsters.

Previous research has highlighted television's potentially harmful effects on children.

It has been blamed for causing sleep disorders, depression, anxiety and violent behaviour.

The study, entitled 'Television: The Public's View', showed that parents who spend more time in front of the TV are more likely to allow their children to have their own set.

Researchers also confirmed that there is a growing trend among parents to use videos and pre-school programmes to keep children occupied.

The Pre-school Learning Alliance warned parents to keep a close eye on the content of their children's viewing and the amount of time spent watching TV.

'Young children require many different types of stimulus to help them develop and learn, and television can be one of these,' a spokesman said. 'But it must be used in moderation and preferably with parental interaction.'

The ITC survey showed many parents apparently do not stop their children watching unsuitable programmes.

Only 47 per cent said they prevent youngsters watching programmes they think are inappropriate. However, this was up from 39 per cent the previous year.

A study last month warned that British children are becoming heavily addicted to television.

Researchers from the London School of Economics said youngsters in the UK watch around five hours of television a day, whereas the average in the rest of Europe is just two hours.

'The UK tends to stand apart as a country where screen entertainment, above all television viewing, is particularly important for children,' the report said.

1 Answer these questions to help you understand the text.

a) According to the article, how many children under four have televisions in their bedrooms?

b) How many have a video recorder?

c) What effect can television have on young viewers? Write down one.

d) What are parents doing, or not doing, that makes the situation worse? List three things.

e) The report says that the UK tends to 'stand apart' as a country where television is particularly important to children. What do you think the writer means by 'stand apart'?

2 Complete these tasks and questions to help you interpret the text.

a) Look at the way the article is written. Why do you think the paragraphs are so short?

b) Why has the writer decided to start the article with a fact about under fours?

c) Look at these three quotations from the article. These phrases would still make sense without the words in italics. Why has the writer used them?
- 'The figure has risen *dramatically*'
- 'the survey raised *serious* concerns'
- 'children are becoming *heavily* addicted'

d) The report gives opinions from four organisations. Why has the writer chosen to include these?

e) Write down a statement from the text which supports the view that television can be harmful.

f) Write down a statement which gives the opposite view.

3 Which of these statements do you think is most accurate? Explain your choice in one sentence.

A The article shows us lots of different opinions, including the writer's.

B The article shows us lots of different opinions, but not the writer's.

C The article shows us just a few different opinions, including the writer's.

D The article shows us just a few different opinions, but not the writer's.

4 If you were the sub-editor of this article, what kind of photograph would you use to accompany the story?

Activity 3 Responding to the article

Imagine that you disagree that television is harmful for toddlers. You think that a TV in a child's bedroom isn't always a bad thing.

Write a letter to the *Daily Mail* setting out your case. Remember that newspaper letters need to be short, so aim to express your view in 100–150 words. Use the advice below to help with this task.

Planning your letter
- Decide on the three key points you want to make in your argument.
- For two of them, think of, or find, some evidence to prove your point. It could be a fact or statistic, an expert's opinion or an example from your own experience.

Writing your letter
Paragraph 1: Explain why you are writing, giving your opinion clearly and forcefully in one sentence.
Paragraph 2: Make your **point**. Prove it with your **evidence**. Then **explain** how the evidence proves your point and backs up your view on televisions in toddlers' bedrooms.
Paragraph 3: Use the same structure as the previous paragraph to make your second key point.
Paragraph 4: Use your third key point to give your overall opinion again, clearly and forcefully.

Improving your letter
Check that you have used powerful, emotive language like the writer of the article on page 139 (*serious, heavily, dramatically*). If not, try to add some.

Assess your progress

Tick your work to show you have done these things.

- I have given my opinion in my first paragraph.   ✓
- I have started my 2nd and 3rd paragraphs with a key point.   ✓ ✓
- I have backed up both key points with evidence.   ✓ ✓
- I have given an explanation in both my 2nd and 3rd paragraphs.   ✓ ✓
- I have made a final point in my 4th paragraph.   ✓
- I have given my opinion again in my 4th paragraph.   ✓
- I have included at least three pieces of powerful and emotive language in my letter.   ✓

If you have fewer than ten ticks, try to improve your letter and get all ten.

2

Looking at the way the effects of television are reported

You will learn:
- about the possible effects of television on viewers
- to look at the way writers present facts and opinions.

Occasionally, newspapers report bad news about television – especially its effects on children. This is an unusual story from Japan, where it was reported that a cartoon show left 600 viewers feeling sick.

Activity 1 Analysing a negative review

Convulsive viewing: 600 children get sick watching cartoon

A television cartoon based on the popular video game Pocket Monsters triggered **convulsions** in hundreds of children around Japan last night when a bright red explosion flashed for five seconds on screens.

A spokesman for the fire department, which carried out a national survey, said at least 618 children suffered convulsions, vomiting, irritated eyes and other symptoms.

The Home Affairs Ministry said 208 people, aged from three up to a man aged 58, were still in hospital with epilepsy-type symptoms more than 24 hours after the showing.

The cartoon Pokemon, aired every Tuesday at 6.30pm, has an audience of millions of children.

The children all came down with symptoms about 20 minutes into the 30-minute-long animation.

The *Yomiuri* newspaper quoted a doctor specialising in epileptic fits saying the symptoms were similar to fits some children are susceptible to when they play video games.

Executives of TV Tokyo, the network that broadcast the programme, said they had been inundated with calls. 'We have to find out all the facts and the actual medical explanation,' the executive said.

The cartoon features some Pocket Monsters characters in a video game produced by the toymaker Nintendo Co.

Kyodo News Service said some children reportedly said they felt bad and had vision problems after seeing Pikachu, one of the most popular characters, flash its eyes red during the cartoon.

Yesterday's programme featured a scene with an explosion of a vaccine bomb to destroy a computer virus, followed by the flashing of Pikachu's red eyes for five seconds.

The cartoon has been broadcast on 37 TV stations nationwide since April and has the highest audience rating in the Tokyo area for its time slot.

Dr Yukio Fukuyama, an expert in juvenile epilepsy, said the bright flashes of light and colour from a television could trigger a phenomenon known as television epilepsy.

He said the seizures, albeit unpleasant, were not dangerous and that spontaneous recovery was the norm, but parents should be aware of the side effects of watching programmes featuring bright flashing lights.

glossary

convulsive having convulsions

convulsions sudden violent movements of the body

1 Answer these questions to help you understand the news story.

a) Look at the opening topic sentence. What does it tell us about 'who', 'where' and 'what happened'?

b) What was the exact moment in the cartoon that seems to have triggered the problem?

c) What effects did the cartoon have on viewers? List three.

d) Where does the article tell us *why* this might have happened?

2 If you were the sub-editor of this story, what image would you use to illustrate it?

3 Look again at the story's headline.

a) Would most readers understand what 'convulsive viewing' means?

b) Using no more than seven words, write a different headline for the story. Try to write it so that it attracts people's attention and draws them into the article.

4 Write down three words, phrases or sentences from the article where you think the writer has tried to exaggerate how dramatic or dangerous this incident was.

Activity 2 Writing a response

Imagine you have always believed that cartoons have a bad influence on viewers. You hate *Tom and Jerry* because it's too violent and disapprove of *Scooby Doo* because you think it might scare toddlers.

Write a letter to the newspaper that published the article on page 142. Set out why you think this article proves that cartoons should not be shown on television. Think of:

- the points you will make
- the evidence you will use to support your ideas.

You might start your letter like this:

Sir

I was interested to see the story reporting more than 600...

You could use the same structure as on page 141.

Assess your progress

How confident are you that you can write to argue? For each of the following statements decide if you are:

- unsure ●
- quite sure ◐
- very sure. ●
- I can write an introductory paragraph. ○
- I know a paragraph can be organised using **Point, Evidence, Explain**. ○
- I can write a **point**. ○
- I can include **evidence** for my point. ○
- I can **explain** how my evidence proves my point and my opinion. ○
- I can write a final concluding paragraph. ○
- I know how to include dramatic, emotive language in my writing. ○

3

Exploring television advertising

You will learn:
- how television advertisements are developed
- how to analyse a storyboard.

Across the country there are specialist production companies who develop television and radio adverts for big and small clients, trying to encourage viewers to notice their name, product or service. This commercial for Anglian Home Improvements was developed by The JMS Group, based in Norfolk and London.

Activity 1 Exploring the brief

Take a look at the brief that JMS were working to.

Client
Anglian Home Improvements (Britain's largest home improvements company, and one of the oldest established – over 40 years).

Campaign
TV, onto 14 satellite and terrestrial channels during Autumn 2006.

Product
Rooftrim (PVCU drainpipes, guttering, barge-boards, soffits and fascias). Client informs us no one has ever bothered advertising this product line before. Surprising, as it is such a big money spinner.

Challenges
A To make homeowners/viewers take an interest in such a 'mundane' subject.
B To make it look good.
C To give viewers a really good reason to do something about it (offer).
D To make them act RIGHT NOW (24-hour response line).

1 Use a spider diagram to brainstorm your own ideas for how you might make the product in the brief above appeal to viewers. Think about who your target audience might be. What would appeal to them?

2 Make a note of the problems you might face in making the commercial.

Activity 2 'Reading' the storyboard

Study the eight-frame storyboard of the finished commercial produced by JMS.

1 a) Look at each frame. What do you think its message is?

  b) Why do you think the commercial starts with images of the elements, rather than the house?

  c) Look at the image of the house in frame 7. Why do you think this house was chosen? What do you notice about it?

2 Who do you think is the target audience for this advert?

3 Why do you think the advertising agency decided to use a male voice-over?

4 Look again at the challenges the advertising agency was given in the brief. Do you think the advert meets the challenges? Write a sentence or two for each one, explaining your answer.

VISION: We see the rain, sun, wind and ice – the effects of the elements in close up.
SFX: Hard driving rain - a little rumbling thunder.
MV/O: Over the years, the exterior of your home is hit hard ...

VISION: Change of atmosphere – we see ice crystals on a window pane.
SFX: Cold cracking sounds – the wind gently whistles.
MV/O: ... by everything the elements throw at it.

VISION: Cut to change of atmosphere – the sun is blazing down out of a hot summer sky.
SFX: Summery/hot sounds.
MV/O: In time it may suffer and start to cost you more and more money.

VISION: Cut to medium shot of a house exterior. We see hints of a fantastic looking Rooftrim system in place. Camera pans across the roofline. Phone number and caveat cuts on.
SFX: Music bed starts.
MV/O: But you can help take that worry and cost away by calling 0800 500 600 today. Anglian Rooftrim is the stylish way to replace your home's exterior timber.

VISION: Cut to c/u across bargeboards.
MV/O: Our highly durable fascias, soffits and guttering can help protect the exterior of your home in all weathers for years to come.

VISION: Cut to another c/u pan across soffits, etc. 'Free' graphic and caveat cuts on.
MV/O: And it's virtually maintenance free making high access painting a thing of the past. Not only that, if you buy Rooftrim this autumn, all your guttering and downpipes are absolutely free!

VISION: Cut to wide shot of house exterior.
MV/O: Which means you're buying beautiful looking, low-maintenance protection for your home and more time for yourself.

VISION: Cut to logo.
MV/O: Call us on 0800 500 600 today and discover how Anglian Rooftrim can help protect your home. Come rain or shine.

Activity 3 Developing a storyboard

Take the idea below and develop your own storyboard like the one above.

RapidWash car wash

Target audience
People who take pride in their car but don't have time to wash it.

Product
RapidWash is a faster drive-through car wash which leaves cars 50 per cent shinier than normal car washes because of new formula wax. It's available at fifteen service stations across the area.

Assess your progress

Ask a partner to look at your storyboard and say what they think the message of each frame is. How successful were you? Use your partner's suggestions to improve your storyboard.

4

Exploring sketch comedy

You will learn:
- about the structure and language of a comic sketch.

Since the 1960s some television shows have used a range of short sketches to entertain their audiences and sometimes to poke fun at people. Shows like *The Fast Show* and *Little Britain* are based on using familiar characters and catch phrases. Earlier programmes like *The Two Ronnies* also used short sketches, often playing with language to make people laugh.

Here's an extract from a classic *Two Ronnies* sketch, known as 'Fork Handles'.

Activity 1 Before reading the text

1 Read the directions that appear *before* the dialogue. Ronnie Corbett (**RC**) is the shopkeeper and Ronnie Barker (**RB**) is the customer. Make a quick drawing to show how the set for the sketch should look. Use arrows and labels to explain your set.

Fork handles or 'Annie Finkhouse?'

An old ironmonger's shop. A shop that sells everything – garden equipment, ladies' tights, builders' supplies, mousetraps – everything.

A long counter up and down the stage. A door to the back of the shop up left. The back wall also has a counter. Lots of deep drawers and cupboards up high, so that RC has to get a ladder to get some of the goods RB orders.

RC is serving a woman with a toilet roll. He is not too bright.

Activity 2 Reading the text

RC There you are – mind how you go.
(Woman exits. RB enters – a workman. Not too bright either.)
RC Yes, sir?
RB Four candles?
RC Four candles? Yes, sir. *(He gets four candles from a drawer.)* There you are.
RB No – fork handles.
RC Four candles. That's four candles.
RB No, fork handles – handles for forks.
RC Oh, fork handles. *(He gets a garden fork handle from the back of the shop.)* Anything else?
RB *(Looks at his list.)* Got any plugs?
RC What sort of plugs?
RB Bathroom – rubber one.
(RC gets box of bath plugs, holds up two different sizes.)
RC What size?
RB Thirteen amp.
RC Oh, electric plugs. *(Gets electric plug from drawer.)* What else?
RB Saw tips.
RC Saw tips? What you want, ointment?
RB No, tips to cover the saw.
RC Oh. No, we ain't got any.
RB Oh. Got any hoes?
RC Hoes? Yeah. *(He gets a garden hoe from the garden department.)*
RB No – hose.
RC Oh, hose. I thought you meant hoes. *(He gets a roll of garden hose.)*
RB No – hose.

RC (*Gives him a dirty look.*) What hose? (*He gets a packet of ladies' tights from a display stand.*) Pantie-hose, you mean?

RB No, 'O's – letter 'O's – letters for the gate. 'Mon Repose'.

RC Why didn't you say so? (*He gets ladder, climbs up to cupboard high up on wall, gets down box of letters.*) Now, 'O's – here we are – two?

RB Yeah.

RC Right. (*He takes box back up ladder and returns.*) Next?

RB Got any 'P's?

RC Oh, my Gawd. Why didn't you bleedin' say while I'd got the box of letters down here? I'm working me guts out here climbing about all over the shop, putting things back and then getting 'em out again. Now then, (*he is back with the box*) how many? Two?

RB No – peas – three tins of peas.

RC You're having me on, ain't yer? Ain't yer! (*He gets three tins of peas.*)

1 Use these tasks and questions to help you understand the text.

   a) How many different items does RB try to buy during the extract?

   b) For each item, note down how many times RC misunderstands and gets it wrong before he realises what RC really wants.

   c) There are two main reasons for these misunderstandings. What are they?

2 Look at the characters the two Ronnies play. Make notes on how you think they should be dressed, how they should speak and how they should behave.

3 At the end of the extract, RC says: 'You're having me on, ain't yer? Ain't yer!' Do you think RB is deliberately being difficult? How can you tell?

4 Here are some ways in which humour has been created in this sketch. Put them in order from the funniest to the least funny.

   A The shopkeeper gets more and more angry.

   B The customer does not mean to annoy him.

   C The shopkeeper is 'not too bright' and misunderstands the customer.

   D The writer has very cleverly used plays on words ('four candles'/'fork handles') to create the misunderstandings.

Activity 3 Writing a sketch

Use the situation below to create a sketch of your own.

A person rushes across town in a short lunch break to a jeweller's shop. They want to pick up a watch they left there to be repaired. The manager of the shop is out and a new part-time assistant is in charge. The assistant thinks the person in the shop is trying to buy a watch. The person gets increasingly irritated because their lunch break is running out and they need to get back to work. What happens?

Assess your progress

1 Work with a partner to produce a performance of your sketch. List up to four ways in which you have tried to create humour.

2 Perform your sketch in front of another group. Ask them to list up to four ways you tried to create humour.

3 Compare your notes with the group's. Did you agree?

5

Looking at a television situation comedy

You will learn:

- about the way television comedies are written.

Situation comedies are set in a particular location such as a holiday camp, a family house or a hotel. *Fawlty Towers* is often considered one of the best of this genre. Written by John Cleese and Connie Booth, the storylines included chaos and confusion. You are about to study an extract from one of these shows.

Activity 1 Before reading

Use a spider diagram to note what you already know about *Fawlty Towers*. Who are the characters? Where is it set? Which episodes do you remember? What do you like or dislike about the programme?

Activity 2 Reading the text

At the start of episode 7, the very bossy and very deaf Mrs Richards arrives at the hotel, Fawlty Towers. Polly and Sybil are working at the reception desk.

The hotel lobby. Things are busy; Sybil and Polly are dealing with the guests; Basil is finishing a phone call. He goes into the office. Mr Mackintosh comes to the reception desk.

Mackintosh	(*to Polly*) Number seventeen, please.
Sybil	(*to her guest*) Goodbye. Thank you so much. (*He moves off; the phone rings and Sybil answers it.*) Hallo, Fawlty Towers ... Oh, hallo, Mr Hawkins ...
Polly	(*giving Mackintosh his key*) I've arranged your car for two this afternoon, then ...
Mackintosh	Thank you. (*He moves off.*)
Sybil	(*to phone*) Well, you did say today, Mr Hawkins.
Polly	(*to Mr Yardley, who has approached the desk*) Sorry to keep you.
Yardley	That's all right. You do accept cheques?
Polly	With a banker's card, yes.
Sybil	(*to phone*) Well we'll have to cancel the order, then ... yes. No, no, five o'clock will be fine. (*She rings off.*) Oh, Polly ... Brenda can't start until Monday so would you mind doing the rooms till then?
Polly	Oh, no, I could do with the money.
Sybil	Oh, good. (*She goes into the office.*)
Polly	(*checking Yardley's cheque*) There you are ... thank you, Mr Yardley.

Yardley moves off. Mr Thurston approaches Polly. Mrs Richards comes in through the main door, followed by a taxi driver carrying her case.

Polly	(*to Thurston*) Oh, hello ... can I help you?
Mrs Richards	Girl! Would you give me change for this, please.
Polly	In one moment – I'm just dealing with this gentleman. Yes, Mr Thurston?
Mrs Richards	What?
Thurston	Thank you. I was wondering if you could ...
Mrs Richards	I need change for this.
Polly	In a moment – I'm dealing with this gentleman.

Mrs Richards	But I have a taxi driver waiting. Surely this gentleman wouldn't mind if you just gave me change.
Polly	(*to Thurston*) Do you?
Thurston	No, no, go ahead.
Polly	(*giving Mrs Richards her change*) There you are.
Thurston	Can you tell me how to get to Glendower Street ...

Mrs Richards has paid the driver, who exits. She turns back to Polly.

Mrs Richards	Now, I've booked a room and bath with a sea view for three nights ...
Polly	(*to Thurston*) Glendower Street? (*Gets a map.*)
Thurston	Yes.
Mrs Richards	You haven't finished with me.
Polly	Mrs? ...
Mrs Richards	Mrs Richards. Mrs Alice Richards.
Polly	Mrs Richards, Mr Thurston. Mr Thurston, Mrs Richards. (*Mrs Richards, slightly thrown, looks at Mr Thurston.*) Mr Thurston is the gentleman I am attending to at the moment.
Mrs Richards	What?
Polly	(*loudly*) Mr Thurston is the gentleman I am attending to ...
Mrs Richards	Don't shout, I'm not deaf.
Polly	Mr Thurston was here before you, Mrs Richards.
Mrs Richards	But you were serving me.
Polly	I gave you change, but I hadn't finished dealing with him. (*to Thurston*) Glendower Street is this one here, just off Chester Street.
Mrs Richards	Isn't there anyone else in attendance here? Really, this is the most appalling service I've ever ...
Polly	(*spotting Manuel*) Good idea! Manuel! Could you lend Mrs Richards your assistance in connection with her reservation. (*to Thurston*) Now ...(*She continues to give Thurston directions.*)
Mrs Richards	(*to Manuel*) Now, I've reserved a very quiet room, with a bath and a sea view. I specifically asked for a sea view in my written confirmation, so please be sure I have it.
Manuel	*Qué?*
Mrs Richards	... What?
Manuel	... *Qué?*
Mrs Richards	K?
Manuel	*Si.*
Mrs Richards	C? (*Manuel nods.*) KC? (*Manuel looks puzzled.*) KC? What are you trying to say?
Manuel	No, no – *Qué?* – what?
Mrs Richards	K – what?
Manuel	*Si! Qué?* – what?
Mrs Richards	C. K. Watt?
Manuel	... Yes.
Mrs Richards	Who is C. K. Watt?
Manuel	Qué?
Mrs Richards	Is it the manager, Mr Watt?
Manuel	Oh, manager!

Mrs Richards He *is*.
Manuel Ah … Mr Fawlty.
Mrs Richards What?
Manuel Fawlty.
Mrs Richards What are you talking about, you silly little man. (*Turns to Polly, Mr Thurston having gone.*) What is going on here? I ask him for my room, and he tells me the manager's a Mr Watt and he's aged forty.
Manuel No. No. Fawlty.
Mrs Richards Faulty? What's wrong with him?
Polly It's all right, Mrs Richards. He's from Barcelona.
Mrs Richards The manager's from Barcelona?
Manuel No, no. He's from Swanage.
Polly And you're in 22.
Mrs Richards What?
Polly (*leaning over the desk to get close*) You're in room 22. Manuel, take these cases up to 22, will you.
Manuel *Si.*
He goes upstairs with the cases; Mrs Richards follows.

1 Look at the opening of the scene, then answer these questions.

a) How does the dialogue (what the characters say) show that the hotel is busy?

b) Why have the writers made the hotel so busy just as Mrs Richards enters?

c) What is the first impression you get of Mrs Richards?

d) What one word gives you this impression?

e) How does Polly react to Mrs Richards?

2 Like the *Two Ronnies* sketch in Section 4 (pages 146–7), some of the humour in *Fawlty Towers* comes from characters misunderstanding each other. Other humour comes from the situation and from the characters themselves.

a) Find some examples of misunderstandings in the extract. Try to explain why these misunderstandings occur.

b) Now look at the whole extract. At which point does it become funny? Try to explain what makes it funny.

c) There are three main characters in this extract – Mrs Richards, Polly and Manuel. Rank them in order of how much humour each character creates.

3 Imagine you are the director of episode 7. What kind of appearance, dress, voice and manner should the character of Mrs Richards have? Write a description for:

- the casting director
- the costume designer
- the actor.

Activity 3   Looking at the whole episode

Look at this synopsis of the whole episode.

A   Mrs Richards, a very deaf and difficult customer, has come to stay at Fawlty Towers.

B   Basil, the hotel owner, has a betting tip on a horse race. He asks Manuel the waiter to put the bet on for him secretly as his wife Sybil hates him gambling.

C   Mrs Richards is very unhappy with her room. It is cold, the bath is too small and the view not interesting enough.

D   Basil's horse wins. Manuel collects the £75 prize money and gives it to Polly to look after.

E   Mrs Richards says she has had £85 stolen from her room.

F   Sybil remembers seeing Polly counting money and presumes that she has found Mrs Richards' £85.

G   Sybil is suspicious and, believing it is Mrs Richards' money, gives it to her. The money is £10 short, so Sybil takes it from the hotel till.

H   A man delivers a vase to the hotel for Mrs Richards and returns her glove, which she left behind in the shop. It has £95 in it.

I   Basil agrees with Mrs Richards that she has already had her money returned, so he can keep her £95. Then one of the other residents reveals that Basil has been gambling.

J   Sybil grabs the money from Basil and he drops Mrs Richards' vase in shock. Sybil gives his money to Mrs Richards to pay for a replacement.

-5 -4 -3 -2 -1 0 1 2 3 4 5

Going badly   **Average**   **Going well**

1   This episode shows how badly things can go wrong for Basil. For each point in the synopsis (A–J), give his life a mark using this measure.

2   Work out which parts of the story happen because of:
- the characters and their relationships with each other
- mistakes that the characters make during the episode
- things that the characters do on purpose during the episode.

3   Which of these two settings do you think is better for a situation comedy? Think about the kinds of characters that can be involved in each setting.
- A hotel
- The house of one the characters

Activity 4   Brainstorming a situation comedy

Which of these settings might make a good situation comedy?
- An old record shop
- A coffee bar
- Backstage in a theatre

Choose one of the settings above or one of your own. Now think of some comic characters. Make a note of what might happen to them. Write up your ideas in a summary using these subheadings:
- Setting
- Characters
- Possible storylines.

Assess your progress

1   Read other students' ideas for a situation comedy. Write down the five most important ingredients for a successful sitcom idea.

2   a) How many of the five ingredients does your sitcom idea have?
    b) Try to improve your idea so that it has more ingredients from your list.

6

Television drama

You will learn:
- how television dramas appeal to a target audience.

The *Doctor Who* television series has been a great success in recent years. First broadcast in 1963, it was cancelled in the 1980s but returned in 2005 with Christopher Eccleston in the title role and Billie Piper as his assistant, Rose Tyler.

Activity 1 Analysing *Doctor Who*

This extract is taken from the beginning of Series 1, Episode 2 (2005). This is Rose's first journey on the TARDIS.

OA INT. TARDIS DAY 3

The TARDIS is in flight. The groan of the engines; underneath, the hump of power, but it's calm; The Doctor's flying well, grinning as he uses the controls; showing off a bit. ROSE smiling, loving it.

The doctor Right then, Rose Tyler. You tell me, where d'you want to go? Backwards or forwards in time, your choice, what's it gonna be?

ROSE Forwards.

The doctor How far?

ROSE One hundred years.

He operates controls. Loving it. Engines lurch.

The doctor There you go. Walk out of those doors, it's the twenty-second century.

ROSE Kidding.

The doctor That's a bit boring though, d'you wanna go further? [...]

ROSE Fine by me.

He operates controls. Engines lurch.

The doctor Ten thousand years in the future. Step outside, it's twelve thousand and five. The New Roman Empire.

ROSE (laughs) You think you're so impressive.

The doctor I am so impressive!

ROSE You wish.

The doctor Right then. You asked for it. I know exactly where to go. Hold on!

And he slams every control going, wham, wham, wham! The TARDIS does a good spin, Rose has to hold on. The Doctor operating the controls like a maestro. Rose still entranced by it all, even as she holds on tight to the console.

And then slam! The Doctor brings everything to an absolute halt. Engines dead, no movement.

Rose straightens up:

ROSE Where are we...?

He's just confident, gestures to the doors.

ROSE What's out there?

He just indicates again, out you go. Rose smiling, a bit scared, goes to the door...

1 INT. VIEWING GALLERY DAY 3 1500

The TARDIS door opens, Rose looks out, then steps out.

A simple, elegant room. [...]

Rose stands forward at a handrail, as she sees: The Earth. They're right above the planet; it fills the lower half of the wide window.

Rose looks at her world, stunned. The absolute beauty of it.

THE DOCTOR [...] This is the year five-point-five-slash-apple-slash-twenty-six. Five billion years in your future. And this is the day ...

(looks at wristwatch)

Hold on ...

He looks up. And the Sun explodes. The star bursts into a fierce red, and with a wooomph! a wave of yellow expands from it – in all directions, expands. The Earth stands proud, occasional waves of thick orange gas rippling in front of it, but leaving it unharmed.

THE DOCTOR This is the day the Sun expands. Welcome to the end of the world.

1   In which different genres could you put *Doctor Who*? What evidence can you find in this extract to support your decisions?

2   *Doctor Who* contains several imaginative and futuristic ideas. But it also includes things that are recognisable from our world and our time. Make a list of any you can find in this extract. Why do you think it is important for a programme like *Doctor Who* to have them?

3   How does the mood or atmosphere change during this extract? Write down a word or phrase to describe the mood:
   ● at the start of the scene
   ● when Rose and the Doctor come out of the TARDIS
   ● from 'He looks up. And the Sun explodes.'

   Then, for each one, explain how that mood is created using dialogue and the directions for the filmed shots.

4   What do you learn about the characters of the Doctor and Rose from the extract? For each person, write:
   ● a **point** about their characters
   ● **evidence** to prove your point
   ● an **explanation** of how the evidence proves your point.

Activity 2   Creating a science fiction programme

Think of an idea for a science fiction series that will appeal to a wide audience. Write a brief in which you describe the main characters, the settings and one or two storylines. Who will your series appeal to and why?

Assess your progress

Swap your work from Activity 2 with a partner. Imagine you are the commissioning editor for a television company. Will you spend a large amount of money turning your partner's idea into a programme? Write to the idea's creator (your partner) explaining your decision.

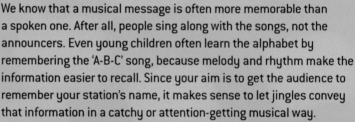

7

Marketing radio

You will learn:
- about the way radio jingles are produced.

There are thousands of radio stations in the UK. So how do they attract their listeners? They try to create a unique image through the jingles they use. These jingles can be sung or they can be sound effects. This section explores the little-known world of jingle production.

Activity 1 Learning about radio jingles

Why use jingles?

Anywhere you go, there are lots of radio signals in the air for listeners to choose from. If you're a programme director, you try to make sure that your station is the best. But no matter how good you sound, it won't do you much good if the audience can't distinguish you from the competition or remember your station's name. Those are major reasons to use a jingle package.

Good jingles help create a unique identity that only your station will have. After all, every station builds its product with the same basic tools: music, information, spots, on-air personalities, competitions and so on. But jingles are one way to put an individual touch to a station's sound. The musical style and attitude of the jingles tell listeners what they can expect from the station. And often a slogan is delivered most effectively in a musical context with a well-produced jingle.

We know that a musical message is often more memorable than a spoken one. After all, people sing along with the songs, not the announcers. Even young children often learn the alphabet by remembering the 'A-B-C' song, because melody and rhythm make the information easier to recall. Since your aim is to get the audience to remember your station's name, it makes sense to let jingles convey that information in a catchy or attention-getting musical way.

And let's not forget that jingles can and should be fun! Whether it's something crazy for the morning show or a romantic sound for late-night dedications, jingles are part of the 'showbiz' magic of radio. They make what you're doing seem more special, just as the curtains, lights and sets do when you're watching a theatrical production.

Read this article about how radio stations try to attract listeners.

1 In the first paragraph, what are the major reasons that radio stations use jingles?

2 How do jingles create an image of the radio station for the listener?

3 Write down three other reasons why radio stations use jingles.

Activity 2 Exploring radio station image

BBC radio offers a wide range of programmes on seven national stations. Each one has a different image and appeals to a different audience. The table on p. 155 shows a selection of what was played on four national BBC radio stations one Friday afternoon.

BBC RADIO 1	BBC RADIO 2	BBC RADIO 3*	BBC RADIO 4
'The best new music and entertainment'	'The most listened to radio station in the UK'	'Classical music, jazz, world music, drama and arts discussions'	'Intelligent speech'
Scott Mills	**Chris Evans**	**In Tune**	**Thinking Allowed**
Beyoncé: 'Irreplaceable' (2006)	**Sister Sledge:** 'He's The Greatest Dancer' (1979)	**Beethoven:** Romance in F, Opus 50	Laurie Taylor talks to one of the world's most eminent legal and political philosophers on democracy, liberty and human rights.
Girls Aloud: 'Something Kinda Ooooh' (2006)	**Madness:** 'Driving In My Car' (1982)	**Puccini:** Crisantemi Quartetto	
The Magic Numbers: 'Take A Chance' (2006)	**KLF:** 'Justified and Ancient' (1991)	**Tchaikovsky:** 'Letter scene' from Eugene Onegin	
Panic At The Disco!: 'I Write Sins Not Tragedies' (2006)	**Indeep:** 'Last Night A DJ Saved My Life' (1983)	**Liszt:** 'Les Jeux d'eaux à la Villa d'Este'	
Robbie Williams: 'Lovelight' (2006)	**Creedence Clearwater Revival:** 'Have You Ever Seen The Rain?' (1971)		

> Radio stations want to get the biggest audience they can. If one station played a mixture of Radio 1, 2, 3 and 4, everyone would listen to it.

1 Do you agree with this statement? Why?

2 Look back at the table. Compare what each radio station played. Who do you think is the target audience for each of them?

3 Look at the radio stations' logos. How do you think the logos are trying to:
- show what each station's content is like
- appeal to the target audiences you identified in task 2?

4 Write a description of a new jingle for **two** of these stations. Think about the music, the words and the kind of voice you would use.

Activity 3 Creating a new radio station

Create two new radio stations – one designed to appeal to you and one designed to appeal to older people. You need to:
- schedule 30 minutes of content (what the listeners will hear)
- design the radio stations' logos
- write a description of a jingle for each radio station.

Assess your progress

Show your plans for an older person's radio station to a parent or carer. Would they listen to the station? How could it be improved?

Writing a radio drama

You will learn:

- how to write a radio drama
- how words and sounds can be used to convey atmosphere and tell a story.

Some people love to listen to radio drama. They like the fact that it allows you to use your imagination to see characters and places. It is also an exciting medium for writers because you can set your play anywhere – on earth or beyond – simply using sound effects and language to transport your listener.

Activity 1 Looking at a radio script

This is part of a horror play. It is about Bill Halliday, a man who does not understand or like children very much. Having taunted and teased the children in his neighbourhood, he gets drawn into a game of hide and seek with them. Tony and Sylvie are among the children.

Tony	We'll count to a hundred.
Sylvie	One.
Tony	Two.
Girl	Three.
Children	Four.
Sylvie and Children	Five. Six. Seven … (*Fade out.*) (*Fade in.*)
Bill	(*in panting whisper*) Damn fool place to hide – behind spare room curtains. Bound to show. Panic, of course. Should have cheated. Slip out through back door, and come back when they give up. Too late now, though. On their way. Mustn't breathe so hard. They can hear a heart beating. All over the house, now, scrabbling and scuffling. Like rats. Sniffing into cracks and corners. Just like rats. What happens when they find …? Here. Alone. He set this up. Dead cunning. No way out … It's a game. Just a game. Laugh, and switch on the lights. The stairs creaked. They're closer. Trying bedroom doors. Are they scattered, or in a pack? Perhaps they won't think to draw the curtains. Perhaps they'll give up and go away. Persistent little devils, though. It's a game. Only a game. Hush now. Hold your breath. They're here. (*Door opens. Scuffling of tiny feet. A whisper which is shushed. Heavy breathing.*)
Child	(*In loud whisper*) The curtains. (*The whisper is taken up by the others. 'The curtain, curtain, curtain …'*)
Tony	Sssh. (*The curtains are drawn.*) (*Bill gasps, then laughs uneasily.*)
Bill	I give up. (*There is no sound from the children.*)
Bill	All of you here? Well, well, well. All together. What's the routine now? Give three hearty cheers? (*He pauses. There is no sound from the children.*)
Bill	You won, didn't you? Why don't you say 'We won'? One of you. Any of you. Say something. Anything.

1 How can you tell that this extract comes from a radio play rather than being written for television, screen or stage?

2 Write down two ways that the writer builds a sense of tension or menace.

3 Think about the impressions made by the characters in this extract.

    a) What impression do we get of Bill? Make notes on a spider diagram.

    b) Bill speaks in very short sentences and phrases. What impression of him does this create?

    c) What impression do you get of Tony, Sylvie and the other children?

    d) How is this impression created?

4 List all the sound effects used. What purpose does each one have?

5 Why would this play be more effective on the radio than on television?

Activity 2 Writing a radio play

Read these notes from the BBC website on writing a successful radio drama.

First thoughts
Radio is an extraordinary medium. A radio play can travel through time and space, between centuries and continents. It can take place in an aeroplane, down a goldmine, on a ship. All this can be done for a fraction of what it would cost to do the same in film. But in every case the audience has to be attracted, and its attention held, by the means of sound alone.

We asked two award-winning radio dramatists, Marcy Kahan and Mike Walker, to share their secrets and to explain what makes an effective radio play.

Themes
You can write on any subject. Your play can be set in the past, present or future.

How to structure a radio play
A radio play has scenes like a stage play. One scene might consist of one line of dialogue, or it might just consist of a sound effect (know as SFX).

Vary the pace and length of scenes, as well as their 'location'. A radio play that has six ten-minute scenes, each set in a dining room, is likely to be less effective than a play that varies its scenes and settings. Drawing in the listener immediately is crucial.

Thinking in sound
A variety of sounds is essential for holding the listeners' attention. This can be achieved by altering the length of scenes, the number of people speaking, the pace of the dialogue and the location.

The contrast between a noisy sequence with a number of voices and effects, and a quiet passage of interior monologue (the actor thinking aloud to themselves) is very effective. There is also a good contrast to be achieved between an indoor setting and an outside setting.

Sound effects
These should be used sparingly. They can be used functionally (e.g. door opening) or to create a mood (e.g. dogs barking in the distance on wasteland).

1 Use these tasks and questions to help you understand the text.

   a) The writer describes radio as 'an extraordinary medium'. Write down one thing he thinks is extraordinary.

   b) What is the difference between a functional sound effect and one used to create mood?

   c) How would you use sound effects to establish the following settings?
   - a school playground
   - a spaceship
   - a busy factory

2 Using the article to help you, write ten bullet points of advice on how to write a radio drama.

Activity 3 Creating your own radio drama

Take the idea below to write an attention-grabbing opening sequence to a radio play in which tension gradually builds. Use sound and dialogue as creatively as you can.

Two people are accidentally locked overnight in the storeroom of a supermarket. They hear noises outside and think it's probably the security guard. Then they start to realise it is burglars.

hint Look back at the work you did on Activity 1 (page 157) and your answer to question 2, Activity 2 above. Remember to set out your drama like the extract on page 156.

Assess your progress

Make a mark on the script you prepared for Activity 3 at each point where you feel you have added to the tension in your play. Check that you have used all of the following to build tension:
- dialogue
- sound effects
- silence.

Use labels and arrows to show where.

Assessment task

The great television debate

You are about to debate whether television is a good thing or a bad thing.

Team selection
Get into groups of four, then divide into two teams of two. One team is going to argue that television is a good thing; the other is going to argue that it is a bad thing.

Training
In your pairs, prepare your arguments either for or against television. You can use some of the ideas and evidence on the next page and add some of your own.

Then, to make sure you are really ready for the debate, think of four or five arguments your opponents might use. Think of arguments to use against them, to show that they are wrong.

The match
It's time to face the opposition. Toss a coin to see which team will present their first point. Then take it in turns to make your case.

The rules
- If any team shouts or interrupts, they are disqualified.
- If any team member decides they have been persuaded to agree with the opposition, then the opposition are declared the winners.
- When one team runs out of things to say, they must submit. The other team has won.

hint Don't just present your arguments in the order you wrote them down. Listen to your opponents' arguments carefully so that you can argue against them and show them they are wrong!

Assessment task

For

TV is a great source of entertainment.

TV keeps us informed about the world around us.

All televisions have an 'off' button.

TV can be educational for viewers of all ages.

Research shows that positive role models and behaviour seen on television have a positive effect on viewers.

TV is company for people who live alone.

TV shows us things and places we would never see without it.

There is no conclusive evidence that TV violence makes viewers behave violently.

Against

Research shows that watching lots of TV during childhood makes you less likely to have a degree by your mid-20s.

Research shows that the average child will have seen 100,000 acts of violence, including 8000 murders, on TV by the age of thirteen.

The average UK child watches too much television: three hours a day.

You're much better off getting some exercise than sitting in front of the TV getting fat.

TV is addictive. The programme you wanted to watch finishes and you just stay there, watching rubbish.

It stops families talking to each other. They eat their dinner in front of it instead of talking round a table.

People don't read books any more – they just watch television.

TV has taken over children's lives. They have no hobbies and no interests any more.

This unit helps you to explore why people love watching films, whether in the cinema, on television or on DVD.

You will learn:

- why watching films remains so popular
- how films are made
- how they are marketed
- how a text is adapted for a film.

6 Film

Getting started

Here are some of the most popular movies of all time, according to visitors of a film website:

Casablanca (1942)
Rear Window (1954)
12 Angry Men (1957)
The Godfather (1972)
One Flew Over the Cuckoo's Nest (1975)
Star Wars (1977)
Raiders of the Lost Ark (1981)
Schindler's List (1993)
The Shawshank Redemption (1994)
The Lord of the Rings: The Fellowship of the Ring (2001)

Write down your top three favourite films, and your least favourite film. They don't have to be from this list.

1

Exploring silent movies

You will learn:
- why silent movies were so popular
- how they were put together.

These days, it's hard to imagine just how magical the very first movies seemed. Even though they were silent they fascinated audiences. The words spoken by the actors were written along the bottom of the screen, and a pianist playing live in the cinema would provide the music. When one early film showed a steam train coming towards the camera, the audience hid behind their seats in panic. The following activities will introduce you to this kind of film.

Activity 1 Learning about silent movies

The text and photographs below outline the beginnings of one place that just about everyone in the world will have heard of: Hollywood.

Hollywood in the silent era

The invention of moving pictures was such a sensation that audiences paid just to see people walking or dancing on screen. When the novelty wore off, New York and Philadelphia film companies built roof-top studios and turned out short, cheap dramas: films that told stories, like stage plays. But for good pictures, they needed sunshine, and they soon became tired of waiting for the clouds over the East Coast to clear. In 1910, many film makers headed west for California. There, close to Los Angeles, they found a sleepy town called Hollywood. Land was cheap, wages were low, the sun shone constantly and there was an incredible variety of background landscapes for their movies, just a short distance away. Hollywood grew quickly – from 5000 people in 1910 to 35,000 less than a decade later. The film people created studios, the studios created movie stars, the stars built mansions, and soon the very name 'Hollywood' came to mean 'movies'.

Florence Lawrence, Hollywood's first star.

Caption cards told the audience what was happening.

It became a tradition to name the chairs of film stars and directors.

The silent camera was cranked by hand.

1 Study the text for Activity 1, then answer these questions.

a) What word would you use to describe people's first reaction to the invention of moving pictures?

b) What three reasons made film makers move to Hollywood?

c) What do you think the writer means by 'soon the very name "Hollywood" came to mean "movies"'?

d) What clues are there that movie stars could earn a lot of money?

2 List the facts about silent movies that you found most interesting.

Activity 2 Telling a story silently

Silent films have to communicate their story very clearly. This is done through the acting, the captions and with the help of live music.

Look at the following outline for a short silent movie.

> A man is walking along a country lane. He comes across a gate to a field, where he sees a signwriter painting on a plaque 'Beware of the bull'. The man looks over the gate and around the field, and decides it is safe. He continues his journey by walking across the field. Suddenly he ducks because people with rifles are shooting pheasants. Keeping his head down he runs back to the edge of the field and sees that the signwriter has just finished the sign. It says: 'Beware of the bullets'!

1 Use a storyboard frame to show how you would tell this story in a silent movie. Would you need to use any caption cards?

2 Under your storyboard write two paragraphs.
- Para 1 should explain how you approached the task.
- Para 2 should describe any difficulties and how you overcame them.

Activity 3 Adding sound to a silent story

Imagine the film you wrote for Activity 2 is being shown in a cinema in the early 1900s. You want to add sound but are going to have to do it 'live'.

1 What will you have to take into the cinema to create the sound effects your film needs? Add notes to your storyboard (Activity 2), showing where each sound effect should be used.

2 Think about the music you need to accompany your film. Remember, you only have a pianist. Will you need more than one style of music? Add more notes to your storyboard, showing where you want the different styles, and where you want silence.

Assess your progress

Imagine you are writing a guide for silent movie makers in the early twentieth century. List the three key things they need to remember when making silent films so that the audience will both understand and enjoy the story.

2

Exploring film language

You will learn:
- about different specialist words used to describe different camera shots
- how you can use these techniques to tell a story.

Although they generally contain speech, films mainly tell their stories through pictures. Just as a writer in a novel might use a range of techniques (such as description, dialogue and suspense), so a film director uses different camera shots. Use the following activities to learn more about these techniques and the language used to describe them.

Activity 1 Learning about camera language

Like most things, film making has its own language, or jargon, as this list of camera angles shows.

Very long shot or wide angle shot (VLS/WAS): this shows the main figure(s) as quite small in the landscape. It gives us a broad impression of where the figure is. It is good for setting a scene.	**Long shot/medium long shot (LS/MLS):** here there is more focus on the figure in the frame. We can see the figure full length, head to toe, as well as plenty of surrounding background.	**Medium shot/mid-shot (MS):** the frame extends down to the figure's waist, so that we can see the figure's expression and gesture in more detail. There could be two figures in this shot, which would be called a 'two shot'.	**Medium close up (MCU):** the figure is framed from just above the head to just below the shoulders. The figure is therefore the main focus, with the background less visible.

Close up (CU): the figure is framed from the top of the head to just below the chin. The focus is now strongly on the figure's facial expressions.	**Big close up (BCU):** there is no background detail at all, just a really close focus from forehead to chin. It is used to show how someone is feeling or reacting to something	**Low angle shot (LAS):** the camera position is low, looking up at the figure or object in the frame. It can be used to exaggerate its size or power.	**High angle shot (HAS):** the camera position is high, looking down at the figure or object in the frame. It can be used to make the figure or object look small or vulnerable.	**Aerial shot (AS):** the camera is high above the action in a helicopter or aeroplane. It is usually used to combine the effect of a long shot and a high angle shot.

1 Choose three of these stills. Write a sentence or two for each, explaining what effect you think the director wanted it to have on the audience.

Activity 2 Using storyboards

Storyboards show a sequence of events, as you have already seen in Activity 2 (page 163). They are often used in the planning process for making films.

1 Look at this idea for a story. Using a storyboard, think about how you would tell the story in film. Underneath each frame write down:
- the shot type (with abbreviations, where possible)
- any sound effects needed
- details of music that will help to create atmosphere.

hint

Aim to give a variety of camera shots. Spend just a brief time on each shot rather than giving too much detail – it's just an impression.

> A boy and a girl are walking home at night through a graveyard. It is dark and misty. They both look a bit nervous. An owl hoots and the boy turns his head in shock. They look across the rows of gravestones and see the exit gates in the distance. The girl says: 'Let's just read some of the gravestones to see who's the oldest person in here.' The camera shows us one gravestone after another. The couple get nearer to the gates, still in mist. The boy looks down at one last stone. He looks confused. He says: 'I can't believe this – someone who lived to 181!' The girl reacts. 'Who was it?' she asks. He replies: 'Says his name was Miles, from London.' The girl looks down at the stone which says '181 Miles From London'. They laugh, hold hands, exit through the gates and skip off up the street.

2 When you have completed your storyboard, write a paragraph saying:
- what you found easy or difficult about the task
- how well you think your film version works.

Activity 3 Creating a leaflet

Some primary school pupils are going to make a film called *A day in the life of our school*. On one side of A4 paper, write a factsheet advising them on:
- the features of their school they might want to show the audience
- the best camera shot to use for each feature.

Remember to explain each camera shot and the effect it has.

Assess your progress

1 Compare your knowledge of different camera shots in Activity 3 with the list on page 164.
   a) Which shots did you NOT include in your factsheet?
   b) Which of the ones you included did you find difficult to explain?

2 Using abbreviations where possible, make a list of all the camera shots on page 164. For each one, decide whether you:
- don't remember it at all
- remembered what it meant when you read it
- understand it and can explain it.

3

Marketing movies

You will learn:
- how movie posters inform us about key features of a film
- how to design an effective movie poster.

How do you decide whether to watch a film or not? In this section, find out more about the way movie posters are designed.

Activity 1 Reading movie posters

Here are five movie posters that have appeared outside cinemas and in newspaper and magazine advertisements.

1 Look at this list of genres (categories of films/books).

Adventure	Romance	Mystery	Horror
Crime	Science fiction	Comedy	

a) Decide which genre best seems to describe each poster.

b) What feature of each poster helped you to decide?

2 Take another look at all the posters.

   a) Which one is the oldest? How can you tell?

   b) Which one grabs your attention the most? Explain why.

3 Look more closely at the poster for *Air Force One*.

   a) What do you think the film is about?

   b) How has the designer made Harrison Ford's face dramatic?

   c) What do you think is the most important element in the poster?

- The actor's name.
- The title.
- The image of the star.

   d) Who do you think the intended audience might be?

- Child
- 16–25
- 40+
- Females
- Young adult
- 25–40
- Males
- Males and females

   e) How do you think the poster could be improved?

4 Choose one of the other posters on page 166 and do a similar analysis to describe:

- how it is organised
- how it uses images and words
- who it might be aimed at.

Activity 2   Creating a poster

Imagine you are a designer. You have been given the following brief.

⊖ ◯ ◯   ◯

Odd One In is a new crazy comedy about a young male/female couple who are asked to babysit a friend's pet for a weekend. What they didn't realise is the pet is a gorilla.

Slogan: 'It was only a weekend but it felt like a lifetime.'

Target audience: 16–24 male/female.

Come up with some ideas for posters using this sequence.

1 Think of two well-known actors who could play these roles.

2 Create three initial designs for the poster, thinking about where you might put the title and the slogan.

3 Think about the image of the couple and the gorilla. What kind of shot will you use? How will they stand? What kind of facial expression?

Remember that the task is about ideas; it's not a finished plan.

Assess your progress

1 Choose your most promising idea for a film poster in Activity 2. Write a paragraph that explains your thoughts and what you have tried to achieve.

2 Ask a partner to look at your poster and paragraph. How successful do they think you have been?

4

Exploring the use of locations

You will learn:
- how film makers use setting to communicate messages about characters
- how the setting for *Shrek* was made.

Because films are visual, the locations and interiors are carefully chosen. Often the backdrop to a character can tell you more about what the character is like. This is especially true in animated and computer-generated films, like *Shrek*.

Activity 1   Exploring locations

Read this extract to learn more about the use of locations. Then answer questions 1–6.

From swamp to screen

Shrek's swamp

When you see Shrek at home in his swamp, then watch Shrek and Donkey enter Lord Farquaard's Duloc Castle, you notice some very big contrasts.

The colours of Shrek's swamp home are all greens, browns and other soft, warm, inviting colours. The lighting is also soft and the atmosphere is homely. The furniture in Shrek's house is home-made and rough, but friendly. The fire gives a gentle glow across the room, The table is full of food, there's a 'lived-in' feel with lots of homely objects and it's all warm, round and comfortable. You feel that Shrek loves the things in his house as much as we love the things in our own bedrooms.

The designers wanted to create a natural look and feel for Shrek's house and the forest around his swamp, without sharp edges or harsh colours. Shrek's world reflects his true character: underneath the surface he is also warm, natural and friendly. Shrek's world is small, but he is big – big in size and with a big heart too.

Duloc Castle

In contrast, the colours of Duloc Castle are harsh whites, washed-out greys and cold blues. The lighting is also harsh and there is nothing soft, round or gentle – everything is angular and sharp, cold and uninviting. The hedges, trees and grass are too perfect, all perfectly cut and unnatural. Even the glass of milk used to torture Gingerbread Man has angular sides – it's not a smooth, round glass. The houses all look the same, there is no individual style or lived-in feel to them. The shop windows are full of souvenir dolls all looking like Lord Farquaad. They are factory made, with no human or warm qualities at all.

This is a very manufactured world, like a theme-park world with nothing looking natural – in fact the entrance to the castle looks exactly like a theme park. The first scene inside the castle reinforces this 'false reality', with the false friendliness of the mechanical doll song, the cold empty streets and the impersonal instant photo.

This all reflects Lord Farquaad's true character as well – cold and calculating, pretending to be what he is not, false and unfriendly. Lord Farquaad's world is big, but he is small – small in size and with very little feeling or warmth.

Real and unreal

These worlds have been created by the film designers and scriptwriters to be an important part of the story itself. Wherever Shrek and Donkey travel, the scenes around them tell the audience a lot about the people and the emotions associated with that place.

Lord Farquaad wants to be a king like the powerful rulers of the Middle Ages. So he has a castle, knights, armour and people who serve him as their lord and master. But his castle has modern ingredients that don't fit the Middle Ages at all – like parking spaces outside the castle entrance, queuing ropes at the castle gates, mechanical welcoming dolls inside the castle, instant photos, recorded music playing over loudspeakers, people holding up applause signs, and a boxing ring.

Putting objects or ideas from a more recent time into the past (or vice versa) is called using **anachronisms**. It's like seeing a digital watch on the wrist of a Roman gladiator in a movie about the ancient Roman emperors. Here the makers of Shrek have placed anachronisms into the story on purpose – for humour, and to help tell the audience the truth about the place and the people who live there.

glossary

anachronism an object that does not really belong in that time period

1 What do we learn about the character of Shrek?

2 What do we learn about the character of Lord Farquaad?

3 What do we learn about the differences in each character's home? Using a table like this one, list five differences.

Shrek's home	Lord Farquaad's castle

4 How does Shrek's home mirror his personality? Explain using your own words.

5 Look at the description of Duloc. What does the writer mean when he describes it as a 'manufactured world'?

6 How do the animators make Duloc seem cold and impersonal?

Activity 2   Creating locations

Imagine you are the scriptwriter or designer for one of the movie ideas below. Think about how you would design the home location.

A *Little Red Riding Hood* – the wolf's den
B *Goldilocks and the Three Bears* – the bears' kitchen
C *Cinderella* – the ugly sisters' bedroom

1 Answer these questions to help you make your decisions.

   a) What kind of personality do you want your chosen character(s) to have? Write down three words to describe them.

   b) What overall impression do you want the setting to give? Write down two or three sentences to describe it.

   c) What might be in the room? (Think about furniture, ornaments, decoration, etc.)

2 Write a sentence or two about the mood you will create with lighting and colour. Will your set be:

- bright or dark
- warm or cold
- welcoming and cosy or foreboding and scary?

3 Produce a series of sketches with notes that explain how your set will look. Produce one sketch that shows the whole set plus lots of close-up sketches to show more detail.

Assess your progress

Show a partner your sketches and notes. Ask them to write a description of your chosen character based on the setting. Discuss with them:

- what they could tell about the character by looking at the setting
- how they could tell
- how the set could be improved.

5

Looking at the structure of film scripts

You will learn:
- how to develop an initial idea into a film script
- how to structure your ideas.

Writing a film script is a specialist job. You need to be able to tell a story through visuals and dialogue, knowing what to say directly and what to leave to the audience's imagination.

Activity 1 Exploring structure

In the text below, South African film-maker Luiz De Barros offers some guidance in writing a film script.

The plot

The first thing is to work out what your script will be about. This is your business, so figure it out yourself – although bear in mind what is written below because it does impact on the type or idea you will want to develop. Then you need to create a plot, i.e. basically what happens in your story and in what order.

The traditional Hollywood script plot structure is often called the three-act structure. Another way of looking at it is what I call the 'balance-imbalance-balance' concept. These concepts work pretty much the same – focusing primarily on a central character. The 'balance-imbalance-balance' structure works in the following way. (We'll call our central character 'X'.)

Act 1, Balance: this is the initial state of your main character.
X is a content dog trainer living with her dog Shoop. She avoids men because of previous affairs gone sour.

Act 2, Imbalance: a challenge or obstacle is forced onto our hero, which she has to do something about. This changes her life.
Shoop is stolen by a rival dog-training company. Lonely and in low spirits, X spends her time searching for Shoop. She begins to lose customers as a result. Along the way she meets a helpful, sensitive policeman who embarks on the dog-searching journey with her. Eventually she and the policeman track down Shoop and rescue the canine.

Act 3, Balance: things are restored back to order but with something gained.
*Having rescued the dog, X returns to her life of contented dog training – but with the addition of her new boyfriend, the policeman. She has also overcome her fear of taking romantic risks. With the help of her new **beau**, her business has taken off like never before. Our hero has learnt something and gained from the experience. In other words, she has developed.*

The most dramatic elements occur in the 'imbalance' section. The challenge and what our hero does to overcome it is the 'meat on the bones' of our story.

If I were to ask what X's primary challenge is, you might say that it is to find her dog. I might disagree and say that her primary goal is actually to overcome her loneliness and fear of men. In this way scripts can have different levels of meaning.

X's story could be a comedy, a serious drama and even a feminist comment on the way women are expected to conform to a **patriarchal** society in which life without a man is seen as meaningless. It's your choice.

glossary
beau
boyfriend
patriarchal
ruled by men

1 Read the text, then answer these questions.
  a) The first paragraph uses the word 'plot'. What do you think it means?
  b) What problems does the character, X, have:
     ● at the start of the film   ● during the film?
  c) Compare X's life at the start and the end of the film. What has changed?
  d) What, or who, has brought about these changes?

2 The writer of the text describes the classic structure of a film as 'balance-imbalance-balance'. Describe what you think this means.

3 Choose three films you know well. Use a table like this one to explore the way they are structured. Did any of the films you thought of not really fit this pattern? Write a sentence or two explaining why not.

	Film 1	Film 2	Film 3
Main idea – in one sentence.			
Main character's hopes/desires.			
Describe the early part of film where there is 'balance'.			
Describe what the imbalance is – what goes wrong in the character's life.			
Describe the final balance – how things get sorted out.			

Activity 2: Structuring your own script

Think of a film script idea that has the structure of 'balance-imbalance-balance'. At the start, your character's life seems straightforward. Then something happens to change it. At the end, your character is different but happy. Think of:
● the setting   ● the main character   ● the main event that changes their life.

Assess your progress

Answer questions 1b–d above using your film script idea. If you cannot answer any of them, you will need to add more detail to your idea.

Writing a film script

You will learn:
- how to write a film script.

In Section 5 (pages 172–3), we read some advice from South African film maker Luiz De Barros on writing a film. Here, he continues his advice. It will help you to understand how you can turn your initial ideas into a script.

Activity 1 Setting out a script

1

Clearly write out your concept in a couple of lines, e.g.:
'This movie is about X, a happy dog trainer whose life is thrown into chaos when her faithful doggy companion Shoop is abducted by a rival dog-training company.'

This sets out what your story is about as well as who your primary characters are. You should also try to figure out if this will be a comedy, a drama or horror story. This is called the genre of the film. No dialogue should be added until Step 7.

2

Write a paragraph outlining the story in a little more detail – this time adding in a few more characters and important events. Get a stronger feeling for how the thing will play out.
We find out X has actually been rather lonely, we learn that there's a hot policeman in there too and there's a climactic shootout towards the end when Shoop is rescued.

One could call this paragraph a short synopsis of your story.

3

Write a longer outline of your plot. Depending on you, this can be anything from 2–20 pages. You can also break this step into more steps and write increasingly longer outlines before proceeding to Step 4. This pretty much establishes the basics of your plot and many of the twists and turns that may take place. Some also call this the 'beats' of your script. You can add in stuff about the bad guys, who they are and their motivation for their actions.

4

Take your long outline and start to break it into one- or two-line paragraphs. Each paragraph should be a particular unique event. Here's an example.
Long outline: *'X is woken up in the morning by Shoop's long tongue in her face. Later X drives to her dog-training school with Shoop panting in the back.'*
This now becomes …
Para 1: *'X is woken up in the morning by Shoop's long tongue licking her face.'*
Para 2: *'X drives to her dog-training school with Shoop panting in the back.'*

5

Fill in more paragraphs to make the story flow well. Add more paragraphs to fill out the story and expand elements that need it. The paragraphs should include more detailed actions on how things happen.

6

Turn these paragraphs into scenes. The concept of a scene is very difficult to explain and almost needs to be intuitively understood. I've never seen an adequate explanation or definition to date. It helps a great deal to read as many scripts as possible to get a feeling for this. Nevertheless, roughly, a scene is an event that happens in a unique place and time. Here's a paragraph description:

'X arrives at the factory and after looking around discovers Shoop's dog leash in the bathroom.'

This could be broken into:

EXT. ABANDONED FACTORY. DAY. X looks up at the front of the abandoned factory. A sign atop reads 'NUWARE TILES'. X walks up to the front door and opens it.

INT. ABANDONED FACTORY FLOOR. DAY. Walking through the dark factory building it becomes clear that there is no one here any more. Rubble and trash are strewn all over the floor.

INT. ABANDONED FACTORY TOILET. DAY. X opens the door to a filthy toilet and looks in. About to walk away, she sees something. A dog's leash. Bending down she picks it up and realises that it is Shoop's leash.

7

Start filling in dialogue as well as more detail under each scene. You should have a first draft completed by the end of this process.

8

There's a corny but valuable saying about writing that goes: 'Writing is not about writing – but about re-writing.' The first draft will almost always be poor. It's in the refining, re-writing, re-plotting and fine-tuning that great scripts get made. Congratulations – you've written a script! Now wasn't that fun?

The most useful advice I can give however is to read as many scripts as you can lay your hands on – either on the Internet or at your local bookstore.

★ **INT/EXT:** this refers to the location of the scene. If it is inside, it is INT (for interior). If it is set outside, it is EXT (for exterior). This should be followed by the location, e.g. ABANDONED WAREHOUSE.

★ **DAY/NIGHT:** this refers to whether the scene occurs during the day or at night. This follows the location.

1 Read the advice that Luiz De Barros gives, then answer the questions.

a) What do you understand by the phrase 'genre of the film'?

b) Why do you think he says: 'No dialogue should be added until Step 7'?

c) What is the main purpose of Step 2?

d) What do you think the writer means in Step 2 by a 'synopsis'?

e) Step 5 advises you to add more paragraphs to make the story flow well. Look at the two paragraphs described in Step 4. What paragraphs would you add between these to help the story flow?

f) What should all writers do in Step 8?

Activity 2 Developing a script

Either think of a new script of your own, or take one of the fairy tales you have already looked at in Section 4, Activity 2 (page 171). Using your script, follow the step-by-step advice to develop a movie script. When you get to Step 3, concentrate on developing just the first scene or two of your film. If you would like to use a different fairy tale, you could choose *Jack and the Beanstalk*.

Assess your progress

Now that you have followed the advice given by Luiz De Barros, how effective do you think it is?

- Check that you have followed each step in his advice.
- For each step, write a sentence explaining how it helped you to develop your script.

7

Looking at a movie screenplay

You will learn:

- how writers tell a story and reveal characters through a screenplay
- how the opening of *Bend it Like Beckham* is written.

One of the most successful British films in recent years is *Bend it Like Beckham*. This section explores a summary of the film plus the opening of the screenplay.

Activity 1 Exploring the plot

Jess dreams of playing football just like her hero, David Beckham, but her family want her to be a nice, conservative Indian girl. When Jess meets Jules and is invited to play with the local women's football team, she is given the chance to make her fantasies become a reality. Pursuing the goal of playing football professionally is in direct opposition to her parents' plans that Jess goes to law school, learns to cook Indian food and settles down.

Jules faces a similar conflict with her mother, who wants her to give up football because she believes it is getting in the way of Jules's ability to marry and have a family. Unlike Mr Bhamra (Jess's father), Jules's father supports his daughter's football ambition from the beginning. The only family member to support Jess in her dreams is her cousin Tony.

Jess faces a conflict between honouring her family, who do not understand her football dreams, and loyalty to her football team mates who share her football dreams but do not understand her family pressures. To complicate the situation further, both Jess and Jules are in love with their football coach, Joe.

1 Read the summary of *Bend it Like Beckham*, then answer these questions.
   a) What does Jess want to do with her life?
   b) What do Jess's parents want her to do?
   c) What do Jules's parents want her to do?
   d) What is the difference in the attitude of their two fathers?

2 Summarise the story of this film in a couple of lines, as in Step 1 of Luis de Barros's advice given on page 174.

3 If you were writing a screenplay of the plot, what would the opening scene be like? How would you immediately grab the audience's attention?

Activity 2: Exploring the screenplay

Here is the opening sequence of the film. Look at the way the screenwriter aims to grab the audience's interest.

COMMENTATOR: David Beckham gets the ball again for Manchester United. He's taking responsibility every time they have possession. This reflects the way he's been captaining England.

He's dominating proceedings, hoping perhaps to get a bit more support as he gathers the ball on this right-hand touchline time after time. And the Old Trafford crowd are warming to the way Beckham is taking over, but the question is, where is the goal going to come from to break down Anderlecht? Will it be Scholes? Could it be Ryan Giggs? Would it be Beckham himself? Because Anderlecht are playing a very controlled game.

This is Radzinski, testing the United defence, and Sylvestre possibly with a chance to break forward on the other flank.

And there's the ball that Beckham really wants.

That looked like a body check, but he shrugged off the defender.

It's a decent cross, and there is Bhamra. It's a fine header, and she's scored!

It's a goal by Jess Bhamra! A superb header, beating the defender, and planting the ball beyond the goalkeeper's left hand. Jess Bhamra makes a name for herself at Old Trafford!

And have we discovered a new star here, Gary Lineker?

GARY LINEKER: That's right. Could Bhamra be the answer to England's prayers? Alan?

ALAN HANSEN: Quick thinking, comfortable on the ball, vision and awareness – magnificent. I wish she was playing for Scotland!

John, have England found the player to relive their World Cup glory?

COMMENTATOR: Definitely, and the best thing is, she's not even reached her peak yet.

We're joined now by Jess's mother.

You must be proud of your daughter.

MRS BHAMRA: Not at all. She shouldn't be showing her bare legs to people! She's bringing shame on the family. Don't encourage her!

©2002 BILB Productions Ltd

Study the text on page 178, then answer these questions.

1 What is surprising about this screenplay as an opening to the film?

2 What is the effect of having real football commentators?

3 Where in the script might the audience realise that this is not a normal football match?

4 How does Jess's mother behave differently?

5 What makes the scene funny?

Activity 3: Rethinking the opening

Look again at the plot summary. Think of a different way that the film could have opened, then write a short extract of an alternative opening scene.

You could look back to Activity 1, question 3 on page 177 and develop your answer.

Assess your progress

Compare your idea for an alternative opening with the actual opening. What is similar? What is different? Think about:

- how the scene grabs the audience's attention
- how the audience might react to the scene
- what we learn about the characters and their problems.

8

Looking at horror movies

You will learn:
• about the genre of horror films
• how to write an information text.

Since the earliest days of moving pictures, cinema audiences have enjoyed being frightened. For some, it's the thrill of seeing their heroes in danger. For others, it's the classic fear of monsters about to attack humans. These activities will help you to explore the 'nature versus humans' horror genre.

Activity 1 Exploring the genre

A genre is a category, or type, of film, book or music. Here is an extract from a cinema reference book. Look at the way it presents information about the genre of horror movies.

CRITTERS

Spawned by man's **phobia** of bugs, bees and birds, the animals-run-amok horror movie sees nature, overrun by pollution and nuclear radiation, take revenge against mankind.

NASTY NATURE

With crazed flapping and savage pecking, Alfred Hitchcock's *The Birds* (1963) launched the nature-gone-mad movie. In *Frogs* (1972) it is mutant reptiles and amphibians that attack humankind, while bears are on the prowl in *Grizzly* (1976). A family is mauled by man's best friend in *Cujo* (1983), when a pet dog becomes infected with the disease rabies. *Jaws* (1975) turned oceans into a fear zone forever, and schools of flesh-hungry fish followed in *Piranha* (1978), *Orca* (1977), and the shark-infested *Open Water* (2003).

INSECTS ATTACK!

The killer bug movie was hatched in the 1950s, as a result of America's fears about atomic power. Giant mutant ants are **spawned** in Them! (1954), while toxic cockroaches set fire to their victims in Bug (1975), and chomp their way through humans in The Nest (1988). Plagues of South American killer bees terrorise in The Bees (1978) and The Swarm (1978), when the delicate balance of nature is upset. Horror also made use of spiders in Tarantula (1955) with mammoth man-eating spiders on the prowl, and famously in Arachnophobia (1990), when spiders invade the USA.

This flowchart follows the various stages of a typical plot for an animal horror movie.

Life is normal.	Example: Everyone's enjoying the sunshine on the beach at Amity Island (*Jaws*).
Something causes normal animals to change into monsters – or dangerous creatures are mistakenly released – often the result of human actions.	Example: Nuclear tests in the desert cause normal ants to mutate into giant killer ants (*Them!*).
Havoc.	Example: Deadly South American spiders take over a quiet American town (*Arachnophobia*).
Someone is brave enough or motivated enough to tackle it.	Example: The head park ranger takes on an 18-foot bear …
The first attempt always fails.	Example: … but a useless park manager and lots of drunk sightseeing hunters make it very difficult (*Grizzly*).
So does the next one, or two, or three.	Example: The bees are immune to the usual pesticides (*The Swarm*).
Catastrophe seems unavoidable.	Example: Donna's husband is away from home; she and her five year-old son are trapped by a rabid dog (*Cujo*).
Catastrophe is avoided.	Example: A fighter squadron napalms the giant spider (*Tarantula*).
Everything is alright now.	With the shark dead, our heroes swim safely back to shore (*Jaws*).

1 Take a look at the text on pages 180–1 and the flowchart opposite, both of which give examples of horror movies.

 a) Name two creature horror movies from the 1970s.

 b) Describe the starting point of the problem in *Cujo*.

 c) What was the fear in the 1950s that led to the first killer bug movies?

2 Think of a horror movie you have seen in which humans are attacked by creatures. Describe in a sentence what happens in the film. Then, in a second sentence, say what you think about the film (how much you like or dislike it).

3 Are there any creatures which you can't imagine ever scaring us in a horror film – for example, hedgehogs or guinea pigs? Try to explain why certain creatures don't lend themselves to scaring us in horror films.

4 Make a list of the qualities that you think an animal needs to make it an effective monster for a horror film.

5 Look at the film posters on pages 180–1. How have the images of the animals been made to look as frightening as possible?

Activity 2 Developing a horror idea

Take one of the ideas below and think of a movie concept.
- wasps that start to attack people in parks and gardens
- a pack of mutant dogs that terrorises a city
- rats that begin emerging from sewers and invading people's homes

Think of:
- a title for your film
- the idea for an opening scene where normal life suddenly starts to go wrong
- who your characters might be and what the setting is
- how you will show normal life, then the first hint of attack.

Then choose two of the following tasks.

A Develop the plot following Luiz De Barros's advice in Section 6, Activity 1 (page 174) up to Step 3.

B Storyboard the opening scene, giving details of camera shots, sound effects and music.

C Write the script for the opening scene.

Assess your progress

Imagine your horror film has been made and is about to be shown nationally in cinemas. Write a film review that concentrates on how good your opening scene is. What are the three main things that make it so effective?

9

Developing a movie pitch

You will learn:
- how to develop a movie idea, then 'pitch' it to producers
- how to use language persuasively.

The process of getting a movie made is a long one. Because film making is so expensive, producers want to make successful movies so that they get their money back. A movie idea is repeatedly tested before it goes into production. The tests help to answer these questions.

- **Will it appeal to its target audience?**
- **Who should be in it?**
- **Will the right actors attract enough people to see it?**
- **Is the idea commercial enough, original enough, too original?**

The first stage is to choose the right script. Writers are given an opportunity to persuade the producers that their script would make a great film. This is called 'pitching'.

Activity 1 Learning about the pitching process

Pitching can be a frustrating process – especially for new writers. Read this advice from Lenore Wright on how to pitch a movie successfully.

Use your genre to sell your pitch

Know the genre of your movie. Movies are sold to audiences by genre. Your pitch audience are interested in how they will market the movie as well as how they will make it. Don't tell them how to market it, just make it clear that it is marketable.

What to include in your pitch

The pitch should be about 10 minutes max. This leaves time for feedback. The initial pitch must answer these four questions.

Question 1: Who is the movie about?
Give the impression the movie centres on **one** character, the most interesting character – the **star**. Movies are star-driven. Even low-budget independent producers hope the unknown actor they cast in the lead will become a star or at least look like a star in this movie.

Question 2: What happens to the star?
- ✦ Include the arena of the story and the basic situation of the star.
- ✦ Tell where the star is (emotionally, physically, mentally) at the beginning.
- ✦ Tell where the star goes (emotionally, physically, mentally) during the movie.
- ✦ Explain where the star ends up (emotionally, physically, mentally) by the climax of the movie.
- ✦ Emphasise the conflicts (internal and external) the star faces.
- ✦ Describe how the star's crisis changes them in some fundamental way.

---

1 Answer these questions to help you understand the key points of the text.

  a) Why should you make the genre of your script clear in your pitch?

  b) Why is it important to focus on the central character?

  c) Re-read Question 2 (What happens to the star?). What is the difference between an internal and external conflict?

2 Think of a film you know well.

  a) What obstacles and adversaries does the star face in it?

  b) Which moments would you choose to describe in detail if you were pitching this film?

Activity 2   Developing a movie pitch

Imagine you have been asked to make a pitch for a film. Start by taking a film you already know. Using Lenore Wright's hints from Activity 1, develop your pitch. How would you sell, say, *Jaws* or *Shrek*?

Draft a pitch that you would present to a producer. It needs to focus on:
- the central character/star
- what happens to the star
- a flavour of key moments/scenes
- why the film would appeal to your target audience.

Language hints

- In using language, think about how you will persuade your listener. You might want to use some short, dramatic sentences and contrast them with complex sentences that give more detail.
- You might want to address your listener directly but get them to imagine that they are part of an audience: *'We see a house in a forest. We hear distant singing. The camera shows us …'*
- Make your descriptions vivid and visual – get your listener to imagine they are actually watching the film.

Alternatively, you might develop a brand new idea – a story of your own that would make a good film.

Assess your progress

Using labels and arrows, show where you have followed Lenore Wright's advice in your pitch. Make a note of any of her advice you have not followed. Use these notes to add to and improve your pitch.

Question 3: What gets in the way?
Highlight major obstacles (inanimate or physical situations). Describe important adversaries (characters) that try to prevent the star getting what they want. These blockers should be worthy opponents, otherwise overcoming them won't be satisfying.

Question 4: What's at stake?
Describe a few dramatic moments in detail. Choose moments involving the star where the conflicts escalate or the crisis becomes more complicated. Make it clear the star resolves the climactic crisis or is actively involved in resolving it.

10

Exploring screen adaptations

You will learn:
- how writers adapt texts for movies
- how to 'read' different type of texts.

One of the most successful screen adaptations ever was Baz Luhrmann's *William Shakespeare's Romeo + Juliet*. He took Shakespeare's play and completely reinvented it in a modern setting. This section includes an extract from Shakespeare's play and an extract from the screen adaptation.

Activity 1 Looking at the original text

Text A is the beginning of Shakespeare's original play *Romeo and Juliet*. The scene is Verona, a town in Italy. Two families, the Montagues and the Capulets, have been arguing with each other for years. Another fight has just broken out between them. Benvolio (a Montague) is trying to stop it.

Text A

Enter BENVOLIO

BENVOLIO
Part, fools!
Put up your swords; you know not what you do.

Beats down their swords.

Enter TYBALT

TYBALT
What, art thou drawn among these heartless **hinds**?
Turn **thee**, Benvolio, look upon thy death.

BENVOLIO
I do but keep the peace: put up thy sword,
Or manage it to part these men with me.

TYBALT
What, drawn, and talk of peace! I hate the word,
As I hate hell, all Montagues, and thee:
Have at thee, coward!

They fight.

*Enter several of both **houses**, who join the **fray**.*

1. How successful is Benvolio in bringing the fight to an end?

2. How does Tybalt insult Benvolio? Write down two examples.

3. This is the first time we are introduced to the characters of Benvolio and Tybalt. What can you tell about the character of Benvolio from this extract?

4. What can you tell about the character of Tybalt from this extract?

glossary
hinds female deer
thee you
houses families
fray fight

Activity 2 Looking at the screenplay

Text B is taken from the shooting script of the film by Baz Luhrmann and Craig Pearce – the script the director and actors work from as they make the film. This scene is set in a gas (petrol) station.

Text B

CUT TO: Benvolio. He screams in desperation:
BENVOLIO
Put up your swords!

Gregory, Sampson, Abra and Petruchio freeze. A moment – then from behind, the unmistakable sound of a gun being cocked.

EXTREME CLOSE UP: The black cowboy boots.

CRANE UP: To find the dark cold eyes and feline smile, of the wearer of the boots. His name is TYBALT; a cigarette is clenched between his teeth and his gun is aimed at Benvolio's head.

TYBALT
What, art thou drawn among these heartless hinds?
Turn thee, Benvolio.

Benvolio, a choked explanation:

BENVOLIO
I do but keep the peace.

A mocking smile.

TYBALT
Peace? I hate the word,
As I hate hell, all Montagues, and ...

EXTREME CLOSE UP: Tybalt's finger squeezing the trigger ...
Suddenly we hear firing from Tybalt's blind side.
Tybalt redirects his weapon, cracking off a single shot at the surprise attacker.

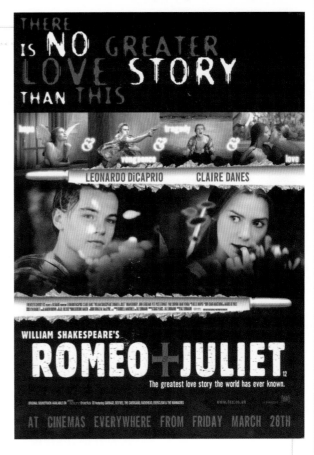

EXT./INT. MINIMART. AFTERNOON.
It is the five year-old from the station wagon. The bullet smacks the toy gun from the child's hand, shattering the wagon's window.
Mother and children scream.

EXT. GAS STATION. AFTERNOON.
A panicked Benvolio falls back, accidentally his gun fires – the bullet whistles past Tybalt's head.

Tybalt combat rolls, and using a screaming car load of girls as cover, returns two quick shots, narrowly missing Benvolio.

EXT. GAS STATION. AFTERNOON.
The gas station attendant hits a button and heavy metal screens slam down.

EXT. GAS STATION. AFTERNOON.
CUT TO: Gregory firing – a bullet rips through Abra's arm.

Petruchio dives for cover; Gregory and Sampson leap into Benvolio's truck.
Rubber burns as they smash past the Capulet vehicle.

CLOSE ON: Tybalt taking aim.

EXT. HIGHWAY – SUPERMARKET. AFTERNOON.
His first shot plugs the fuel tank, the second a tyre. Out of control and spewing gasoline, the Montague truck careers across the highway and through the glass front of a supermarket.

Gregory and Sampson throw themselves from the truck moments before...

EXT. SUPERMARKET. AFTERNOON.
CLOSE ON: The gas tank erupts into an almighty fireball.

1 Read Texts A and B together and start to compare them.

a) Look at the dialogue in both Shakespeare's original and the shooting script. What do you notice?

b) How do the directions in the shooting script show the character of Tybalt?

c) How do they show the character of Benvolio?

d) Compare the stage directions given by Shakespeare with those in the shooting script at the same point. What do you notice?

2 Why do you think the writers of the film script included a mother and son in the fight scene?

3 Why did they choose to set this scene in a gas station?

Activity 3 Reading the images

If you can, watch Act One, Scene One (the gas station scene in Text B) from Baz Luhrmann's film. Use these questions to explore some of the director's decisions.

1 In the first shot of Tybalt, captioned 'The Capulet boys', the camera focuses in close up on his boots. Why do you think the director has chosen to do this?

2 The second shot of Tybalt shows him lighting a cigar. Why is this another unusual shot to choose when introducing a character? What effect does it have – remembering the setting of this scene?

3 Look at the shot which introduces us to Benvolio, captioned 'Benvolio Montague, Romeo's cousin'.

a) How does the composition (or organisation) of the shot affect our view of the gun?

b) What does Benvolio's expression tell us about his feelings?

c) What do the gun and his expression together in this shot tell us?

4 Just after Tybalt has insulted Benvolio, the director uses an extreme close up first of Tybalt's eyes, then of Benvolio's. Why has he chosen to do this?

5 At the end of the scene, the gas station is on fire. The shooting script says that a car crashes into a supermarket and its 'gas tank erupts into an almighty fireball'. In the film, however, Tybalt's cigar sets spilt petrol alight. Why do you think the director changed his mind during filming? Do you think he made the right decision?

Assess your progress

Summarise the main changes made by the screenwriter and the director between the original play, the screenplay and the final images from the film. What similarities and differences do you notice?

Assessment task

Activity 1

This is the opening of a novel, *Montmorency*, by Eleanor Updale. Read it,
then answer the questions that follow to help prepare you for Task B.

The pain woke him again. Not the constant throb that was so familiar he
could hardly remember being without it. This was one of those sharp
stabs from the wound along his thigh. Doctor Farcett had dug deep to
get through to the shattered bone, and the layers of catgut stitching
5　pulled as the torn flesh struggled to realign itself inside. After so many
interventions by the keen young medic, Montmorency should have
been prepared for the agony, but each time the after-effects seemed
worse, and the limited pain relief (alcohol, and the occasional treat of an
experimental gas) less effective.

10　The candle on the central table had burned almost to nothing: it must
be nearly morning, but there was no sign of light through the bars high
up in the wall. Montmorency knew there was no point in calling for the
night guard. Marston, silent, still, and unsmiling, saw his duties in the
prison hospital as strictly limited to preventing escapes. Never mind
15　the fact that Montmorency couldn't even turn over in bed, let alone run
away. He'd have to wait in the dark for the arrival of Nurse Darnley, a
brusque but well-meaning woman who believed that bad people could
be made good and that providing a sip of water to a sick criminal might
help that process.

20　In the meantime, as so often, Montmorency's memory threw up images
from a year ago, of the night he was caught. He had hopped across the
roof of the factory like an animal fleeing for its life. If he hadn't clung
on to the bag of stolen tools, he might have seen the skylight window
before his feet found it and he'd fallen through on to the hard iron frame
25　of the grinding machine. He remembered the cold impact of metal
against his skin, but nothing else until he'd heard people talking about
him as if he wasn't there.

'I can assure you there will be no drain on hospital funds. I will provide
all necessary equipment and supervision.'

30　It was a voice he later recognised as that of Robert Farcett, the surgeon
who wanted to make a name for himself by saving Montmorency from
his multiple injuries.

Assessment task

Montmorency could only imagine what had happened in the interim. No doubt the police, finding his distorted body in the factory, had been
35 delighted that he had got what he deserved for his crime. A quick death would save the courts the trouble and expense of dealing with him. But he had defied their expectations, and his mangled body had been carried off to the teaching hospital near the bridge, where Doctor Farcett had seen him for the first time. The injuries had been grievous,
40 but the body around them had clearly been athletic and strong.

Farcett was preparing a paper for the Royal College of Surgeons on the treatment of complex wounds. He had considered travelling to the Balkans, to find casualties of war so that he could illustrate his theories with real examples. Now, as he worked late amongst the puking poor of
45 London, an ideal subject lay before him. Without Farcett's help, the man would surely die. If he lived, Farcett's reputation might live on too.

1 Write down the names of the characters we are introduced to in this extract. What do we learn about each of them?

2 Where is this opening set?

3 What details are we given to describe the setting?

4 What were the events of a year ago, described in lines 20–29?

5 How did the events of a year ago lead to the events being described now?

Activity 2

1 Write a script for the opening scene of your film adaptation of *Montmorency*.
You will need to decide:
- how much dialogue to include in your script – there is very little in the novel extract but adding more may be a good way to help the audience get a first impression of the characters
- the order of events for the opening (will the events of a year ago appear as a flashback, or will you show them first and then move to a second scene, one year later?)
- what the sets or locations will look like; describe them in detail in your script.

2 Produce a storyboard showing the first eight shots of your opening scene. Remember to give details of the camera shots and sound you want in your film. You can use labels around your drawings if it makes your storyboard clearer.

Glossary

This section has been designed to help you understand specialist media terms so you can use them when you write about the texts and products you study.

broadsheet   newspaper **format** describing large newspapers that traditionally report serious news and political stories; compare with **tabloid**

casting   process of choosing actors to appear in a film or TV programme

cinematographer   person responsible for photographing a film

composition (visual media)   how different elements of a film, TV programme or photograph are arranged for maximum impact

context   time, place or period in which a media product is set

conventions   unwritten rules about genre or text types (e.g. travel writing often uses lots of descriptive language)

design brief   short written outline giving instructions to a design team about the aims of an advertising campaign or other product

director   person responsible for the creative interpretation of a script/story, and the supervision of its filming and **editing**

editing   process of selecting and arranging the right images, words and shots for newspapers, television and film

format   overall concept of a radio station's sound (includes factors like music, news, personalities and **jingles**) or newspaper/magazine layout

jingle   recorded singing of an advertising slogan or radio station name

logo   image or symbol used to make a product or brand more memorable

multi-media   computer technology that allows text, sound, graphic and video images to combine into one programme

narration   scripted **voice-over** commentary, read by a narrator or participant in a film

point of view (POV)   telling a story (in print or film) from the point of view of a particular character

print media   newspapers and magazines

producer   person who plans, co-ordinates and supervises the overall production of a film, including personnel and budget

production manager   person responsible for the shooting schedule and for solving problems on location during filming

propaganda   one-sided information and opinions intended to persuade people to accept or reject a certain idea

screenplay   dramatic script for a film or television programme that includes both dialogue and action descriptions

SFX   special effects or devices to create visual illusions

shot   single image taken by a camera

spin-off   TV programme or video game based on the ideas or characters from another source

tabloid   technically, a publication that is half the size of a standard **broadsheet** newspaper page; sometimes describes newspapers that cover celebrity- and gossip-based stories

target audience   specific groups of people that media **producers** or advertisers want to reach

voice-over (VO)   voice or commentary recorded for use on a film or programme's soundtrack

Heinemann is an imprint of Pearson Education Limited, a company incorporated in England and Wales, having its registered office at Edinburg Gate, Harlow, Essex, CM20 2JE. Registered company number: 872828

Heinemann is the registered trademark of Pearson Education Limited
© Geoff Barton, 2007

First published 2007

15 14 13 12
10 9 8 7 6 5 4 3

British Library Cataloguing in Publication Data is available from the British Library on request.

ISBN: 978 0 435761 88 2

Designed and typeset by Kamae Design
Cover design by Kamae Design
Printed in China (GCC/03)
Cover photo: © Corbis
Picture research by Andreas Schindler at Zooid Pictures Limited

Original illustrations © Harcourt Education Limited, 2007
Illustrated by Phil Healey, Peter Lubach, Mark Ruffle, Rory Walker and Kamae Design

Acknowledgements
The author and publisher would like to thank the following individuals and organisations for permission to reproduce photos:
Album/AKG – Images p. 162 top; Allstar Picture Library/Alamy p.42 right, p.64 left; AKG – Images p.162 bottom right; apex/Apex Photo Agency pp.10-11; Bettmann/Corbis UK Ltd p.57; Cathrine Wessel/Corbis UK Ltd p.24; colinspics/Alamy p.108 top; Content Mine International/Alamy p.43 bottom; Corbis pp.35, 40-1, 104, 108 bottom, 137, 162 centre bottom; c.Sci-Fi/Everett/Rex Features p.152; Dave Hogan/Getty Images p.154; Dan Sinclair/Zooid Pictures p.16 bottom; David Gowans/Alamy p.108 left; David Hosking/Frank Lane Picture Agency p.85; Dinodia Images/Alamy p.42 left; Douglas Slone/Corbis UK Ltd p.172; Dr. Val Kolpakov pp.116-7; Entertainment Film Distributors/Samuelson Productions/VIP4/UKFC p.106; Erich Lessing/AKG – Images p.96 bottom left; Flip Schulke/Corbis UK Ltd pp.60, 96-7 bottom; Getty Images/PhotoDisc /31079 p.5; Getty Images/RubberBall Productions pp.132-3; ImageState/Alamy p.124; Intel Corporation (UK) Ltd p.47; John Robertson/Alamy p.109; Jules Selmes/Harcourt Education pp.8-9; Leonid Nyshko/istockphoto p.120; Liam White/Alamy p.50; Marco Secchi/Alamy p.16 top; Mary Evans Picture Library p.44; MGM/Ronald Grant Archive pp.166 top left, 166 top right; Moviestore Collection Ltd pp. 149, 168, 176-7 bottom, 179, 187; Niall McDiarmid/Alamy p.38; Orban Thierry/Sygma/Corbis UK Ltd p.32; PA/Empics p.67; pfd p.91; PhotoDisc pp.139, 140; Pictorial Press Ltd/Alamy pp.96-7 top; Popperfoto/ Alamy pp.30, 68, 98-9; Powered by Light/Alan Spencer/Alamy pp.12-13; Redmond Durrell/Alamy p.52; Reg Wilson/Rex Features p.146; Richard Young/ Rex Features p.64 right; Romulus Films/Ronald Grant Archive pp.166 left; Ronald Grant Archive pp.161, 162 left, 166 bottom right, 166 left, 169, 176 top, 180 top, 180 bottom left, 180 bottom right, 181 right, 181 left; Science & Society Picture Library p.114; Sipa Press/Rex Features p.17; The Advertising Archives p. 136; Themba Hadebe/Associated Press/Empics p.62-3; Zooid Pictures pp.110, 111.

Every effort has been made to contact copyright holders of material reproduced in this book. Any omissions will be rectified in subsequent printings if notice is given to the publishers.